The Secrets She Kept

Trisha Moriarty

Large Print Edition

Published and Distributed by

COT Publishing

P.O. Box 3379

Myrtle Beach, South Carolina 29578

First printing 2014

Large print edition 2020

Printed in the United States of America

For Maura, Erin, and Shannon

*There is no greater agony than bearing an untold
story inside you.*

Maya Angelou

ACKNOWLEDGMENTS

Special thanks to my beta readers, authors GeorgeAnn Jansson and Trilby Plants.

I am grateful for the continued support and encouragement from the members of the Coastal Authors Network of Pawleys Island, and the Carolina Forest Fiction Writers.

Without the efforts of the staff at the Belchertown Public Library, and the Deputy Assistant Commissioner, Victor Hernandez, of the Massachusetts Department of Developmental Services, this memoir could not have been completed.

PROLOGUE

My dance with my mother ended before the music stopped.

When my nineteen-year-old sister, Hannah, called in the middle of the night, to say that Ma was in the Hitchcock Hospital, and the doctors didn't know what was wrong, the fact that she was still alive was news to me. Certainly, that she was alive and living near my sisters back in Massachusetts, was shocking. Even at only forty-nine, her battle with alcohol surely would have ended. Hannah was not sure how to tell me that Ma contacted her a few months earlier, asking to see her new grandson.

I had put her out of my mind when I moved away. She had left my heart years earlier.

"If you think you'll fly in, we'll hold the body a couple of days longer," Hannah said, when she called the next morning. She was still at the hospital with our twenty-one year-old sister, Connie. They were making final arrangements for the wake and funeral. Ma was dead.

As the oldest child, I completed those same arrangements for Dad, before I moved two years earlier. Forty-nine must be the ultimate age for dying in our family. That fact cautioned me to carefully consider what I wanted to accomplish with the next twenty-four years of my life.

Maybe if Ma was around to help me with Dad's funeral. Or with Hannah's wedding four months later. If she had just been there for my sisters those final years of Dad's bout with Hodgkin's Disease, while they tried everything just to keep him comfortable, without failing their high school classes. Her affair with our parish priest destroyed all our lives. Her disappearance remained a mystery.

My current life existed three thousand miles southwest, in San Diego, California. It would be easy to blame my husband for my hesitation to fly across the country to attend Ma's burial services. He certainly made it clear that he couldn't leave his new assignment and didn't want to be left with two pre-kindergarten daughters, and the responsibilities attributed to daycare, play dates and ballet classes, while running a new company.

There was also the fact that my youngest daughter, who would soon celebrate her third birthday, was being poked and prodded every other day by a group of experts at the Salk Institute, down the canyon in LaJolla. Their attempt to correctly diagnose her mysterious rash was still ongoing. I felt it should have been a simple task for an organization that discovered a vaccine for Polio.

Besides, there was no time to get prepared or to make multiple casseroles that could lie in wait in the freezer, or arrange for neighbors to exchange carpool days, so that everything could continue to run smoothly. I was an expert at making things run smoothly.

But, whom was I kidding? None of those reasons should have kept me from one final viewing of the woman I hadn't seen for nearly a decade. After all, she was my mother. Didn't everyone rush to the side of their mother's coffin? Wasn't that an unspoken agreement between you and the woman who held you in her womb for nine months?

As far as I knew, no one had seen nor heard from Ma, since the day before we buried our father and found her signature on the guest register in the funeral home. She had gone in while we were at dinner and placed her wedding ring in the quilt-lined mahogany box with him.

Years later, I heard that she was actually upstairs in the

the choir loft when we all processed down the aisle behind Dad's coffin for the funeral Mass.

But, as for Ma's funeral…..I was a no show.

CHAPTER ONE

1959 – Hitchcock, Massachusetts

The hot wax was burning my ankle as it dripped down my leg. Replacing the used votive candles on the display rack in the downstairs chapel of the church, with fresh new ones, was a weekly responsibility of mine. Inevitably, I would tilt a candle or two during the replacement process and end up with an ankle in need of first aid cream. It was while I was sitting in the first pew, applying the cream, that I saw Father Blanchard. He was discussing the upcoming celebration with our choir director.

"I'm not sure two processional hymns will be enough," he questioned her, loud enough for anyone praying in the first ten pews to overhear.

There was a buzz around town for weeks with the anticipation of the new priest we were expecting at St. Mary's parish.

"I think everything is falling into place just fine, Father," the choir director responded, as she continued to work on connecting the organ to the tower bells. A job more suited to someone wearing a muscle shirt, if you asked me.

I thought they were acting a little over the top. But high school sophomores weren't supposed to have opinions about things like that. And besides….girls were positioned fourth in the pecking order the Catholics kept……priest, nuns, altar boys, and the lowest of all parishioners….. girls.

Most girls belonged to the choir from the age of being able to sing a note. Because we weren't able to be altar boys, I preformed the necessary chores in the bowels of the church to keep things running smoothly. However, the only reason any of my opinions mattered was because of my heritage. My family name was Newton.

As far as the church was concerned, the Newtons placed high on the list of credible voices in the parish. Not because we had superior theological knowledge, but because we were involved with just about everything that happened in and around the church, school, convent and rectory.

It began at the top with our patriarch. After my grandfather retired from his job delivering heating oil, he became a volunteer maintenance man on the church grounds. When he had a heart attack and died working in the boiler room of the church, no one thought it was an unusual place for him to breathe his very last breath. It was his dedication to the workings of the church that filtered down through the generations and took up residence in my five-foot-one-inch body.

As we waited for the arrival of a new parish priest that fall, my father was the President of the Holy Name Society, my mother was President of the Women's Sodality, and I was on the executive board of the Junior League of Mary. Some might even say we were overly involved in the activities of the church. The new priest would be the spiritual director of all three organizations. The Newtons would know him well.

The gossip in the neighborhood continued to grow with rumors about this Reverend Fitzroy Brennan, due to arrive in time for Sunday's eleven o'clock Mass. There was standing room only by ten forty-five as the choir sang "Mother Beloved," in perfect harmony and volume. It wasn't easy to overpower the great pipe organ or the bells that rang out strong and could be heard across the canal in Morrisville. This would be a Solemn High Mass to beat all. I noticed two women in the second pew, wearing lace mantillas and matching gloves, placed markers in their Mass books, in anticipation of the service. Everywhere I looked, I saw excitement on the faces of the parishioners. Our church was reminiscent of an ancient cathedral, with spires rising above the nave in the center, that were built sixty-two feet higher than the pews. That meant the echo of a crying baby could be heard over any bells that might ring out during the offertory. St. Mary's Catholic Church, at one time referred to as the most beautiful in Hitchcock, was only one of several parishes with elementary schools on their properties, beginning with kindergarten. And it was one of four that went further to educate Catholic children through the twelfth grade. It was located in our section of the city, referred to as Ward 7, more commonly known as The Knoll.

The sun, that morning, streamed through the stained-glass windows and competed with the lit ten-foot-high candles on both side altars.

One honoring the Blessed Virgin, the other, the Sacred Heart. Each of the side altars offered several rows of votive candles, on graduated shelves. In front of kneelers that just stood in ready for parishioners' petitions.

The choir concluded and the organ swelled as all thirty-six altar boys processed out of the sanctuary to take their places on the altar. Their hands were clasped in the praying position as they swayed in step to the instrumental. They wore white cassocks covered with red smocks. After bowing in front of the altar they took seats in chairs that lined the railing.

Father Blanchard and Pastor O'Malley followed behind and took their seats on the second tier of the side platform, leaving an empty seat at the top of the riser.

Within seconds, Father Brennan came across in front of the altar, bowed his head, and continued toward the other priests, rising higher each time his foot went from the back of his heel to the top of his toe. When he reached the highest riser, holding the throne-like chair, an audible gasp was heard throughout the congregation. People in the back pews stepped up on their kneelers to get a better view. You could tell he was pleased with his reception. There was no question about his appearance. He was clearly drop-dead gorgeous. He looked like that famous actor, Robert Goulet. His jet-black hair was curly, and he wore it piled high in a pompadour. His skin was pure white and there wasn't a blemish to be seen. It looked like his smooth newborn baby's skin hadn't changed at all over his thirty-seven years.

The music stopped and all three priests moved up to the altar. The High Mass began.

We could all recite the refrains and responses verbatim. In Catholic schools, we memorized everything in the Baltimore Catechism. Everyone could recite, "God is all knowing, all loving, all just..." So even though the Mass was said in Latin, there was no need to look down at our Mass books.

All eyes followed young Father Brennan as he moved from one side of the altar to the other and up into the pulpit. The most talked about part of his first Mass was his sermon. I don't think anyone could tell you what he spoke about, just how he spoke. Or should I say, acted out. And how his body moved back and forth with his arms stretched out at his sides. It was a performance worthy of a Hollywood Oscar.

When it was time to receive communion, his line of men, women and children stood much longer than the ones leading to the other two priests offering the body and blood of Christ. When the Mass ended, people remained in their pews until all the occupants on the altar moved back into the sanctuary. He was last. That was a first for the parishioners at St. Mary's, at least for as long as my fifteen- year membership.

The congregation moved slowly toward the back of the church, then gathered outside in several small groups at the bottom of the stone steps. They even lingered longer than usual that morning. Walking through the crowd, I overheard comments about his first appearance in our mill town of Hitchcock, Massachusetts.

"What a voice," and "Where do you think he's from?"

The locals were a proud bunch and having someone who looked and preached like Father Brennan only added to their pride. From that morning on, Reverend Fitzroy Brennan would be referred to only as Father Fitz. They liked what they saw and wanted to make him their own.

St. Mary's parish was known for being one of the richest in the diocese, after initiating the first Catholic gambling program. The lottery was called "A Monthly Offering," and it permitted people to attend social affairs and drawings for prizes without the need to pay taxes on their winnings.

It was common knowledge and well publicized around the Western Massachusetts area that St. Mary's parish had found a way to raise large amounts of money without penalty. Soon organizations, like the Knights of Columbus and the Order of Hibernians, were using the same method for their fundraisers. Surely, the money could not have been the reason that attracted this new priest to our parish.

The mystery around his arrival grew. No one seemed to know what parish he came from, or anything else about him for that matter. It wouldn't be long, however, before he was well known – especially to the Newton family.

CHAPTER TWO

If you used the footbridge at the top of Beach Street to walk over the railroad tracks, and went down the forty-six stairs, you found yourself in South Hitchcock, at the bottom of the hill. Canals ran all the way down to Main Street. These waterways were responsible for the many paper mills that employed the majority of our residents. In fact, at one time, Hitchcock was referred to as the Textile Capital of the World. The new houses along the perimeter of Center and Grove Streets were built specifically to house factory workers.

The dam controlling the canals was built by Irish immigrants' hands which allowed the textile industry to thrive. On the first two efforts to build a working dam, they used wood. Both attempts failed. The third time they used granite. There were twelve gates to control the depth of the canals they wanted opened at any given time, depending on the season and number of mills in use.

The Knoll of Hitchcock, our area of the city, attracted Catholics, most of whom had either Irish and/or French backgrounds. My father was one of seven children born to Charles and Anna Newton. His father's ancestors in Canada changed their name from Villeneuve because they thought it was too ethnic. I would have given anything for a little ethnicity when I was in high school being asked, "Hey Newton, how 'bout showing me your figs?" My mother was a Sheehan and told us she was an only child.

Most people living on The Knoll were blue-collar workers with strong family ties, and lives that revolved around the church. The Newton family epitomized the flock.

The majority of Dad's brothers and sisters lived within two or three blocks of one another. Every Sunday after church we went to Granny Newton's for the weekly family dinner. We could always smell the big slab of roast beef in her oven as we walked up the hallway stairs. I still have visions of opening the door and seeing her standing over the stove, wearing her flowered housedress and matching apron. When the weather got warmer, she would roll down her nylon stockings just below her knees. I suppose it was her way of staying cool in the small apartment with a large crowd of hungry relatives. Her long gray hair – I'm sure it wasn't always gray – was rolled up around the crown of her head and pinned in a fashionable bun. She was the center of our world and certainly admired as much by her offspring as Tony Soprano was by his fictional Italian gang.

The adults ate in the large kitchen of her second-floor tenement apartment, and all of us grandchildren ate around a makeshift table in the room most people used for a bedroom. It was the one just off the kitchen. There wasn't one of us enjoying our mashed potatoes and gravy that didn't pine for the day when we'd be old enough to make it to the big table in the kitchen.

With so many Catholic high schools in the city, and just over five thousand parochial students spread out from kindergarten through twelfth grade, the class sizes were quite small. That led to a lot of cliques. There were, of course, the football cheerleaders who walked around the halls in sort of a rhythm. Then there were the really popular girls who always got asked to the dances. They spent most of their weekends shopping downtown at Stearns Department store for the proper attire to wear to the next social.

I always seemed to hangout with Maureen O'Reilly and Norma Hammond. We didn't fall into either of the above categories. We all lived on Beech Street and it seemed natural that as Maureen walked by Norma's house, they should continue down the street together until I joined in as I left my house. At the end of the street, we crossed over to the entrance to the school grounds.

Maureen was very tall and thin, reminiscent of Popeye's Olive Oyl. Norma, in today's society, would be considered a plus size. Back in the fifties, they just called her fat. I was often placed at the front of a school procession because I was one of the shortest girls in my class – not much taller than a hobbit. I was also so skinny I was made to drink malted milkshakes to try to gain weight. I avoided wearing sleeveless blouses because my arms were too thin. Even drinking those shakes after school at Clancy's drugstore soda fountain didn't help the situation. It was years before I was comfortable enough with my weight to feel normal. On my wedding day, I sported a hefty ninety-eight pounds and wore a size three dress. Even then, it needed to be altered to fit better. Today, women pay big bucks to get down to that size. I might be willing to take out a second mortgage to get that former physique myself.

By the time we were teenagers, most of us were smoking at least a pack of cigarettes a day. As a member of the Lucky Strike Club, I was proud to have that red cigarette logo pasted on my notebook. Of course, we had to hide them from the Nuns. Holding them close to our chests usually prevented them from having any reason to use their famous rulers. It was bad enough responding to their clickers and pitch pipes. By the time we got into high school, we had pretty much figured out how to avoid most of their measures of discipline, especially their favorite staple of head slapping.

Almost all of our mothers stayed at home. It was the man's job to bring home the bacon and support the family. Wally and The Beaver wouldn't expect their mother to be at work when they arrived home from school and neither did we. In fact, I even went home for lunch because I lived so close to the school grounds. Ma would be listening to Stella Dallas on the radio during my elementary years. The brown square box sat on top of the ice box in the kitchen allowing us to hear every word as I ate my peanut butter and marshmallow sandwich, and Ma drank a cold beer and smoked one of her Winston's with the filter.

After we got our own television set, Ma was glued to the McCarthy trials. Blacklisting celebrities caught everyone's attention. You could always tell how worked up she got from the coverage of the trial by the number of cigarettes in the ashtray. When the trial ended, I got to use my after-school time period to watch American Bandstand with Dick Clark. My favorite dancers were Justine and Bob, and I spent hours in my room trying to master some of the steps they seemed to find as natural as walking.

Ma went out most evenings with her girlfriends, Liz and Jo. Dad was usually at home to see that we finished our homework. This was not the lifestyle of the Cleavers, but it was my reality. My ten-year-old sister, Connie, seemed to always have her work completed before being queried. Of course, 5th grade assignments certainly didn't require the same degree of difficulty as those from my 10th grade instructors. And my youngest sister, Hannah, had all she could do to master her 3rd grade math assignments. Hannah and I were usually the last to get Dad's permission to leave the table and watch whatever television was left to be seen before bedtime.

Because Ma didn't have a driver's license, her evening excursions would take her somewhere close by in the neighborhood. That usually meant a bar. They were plentiful in the city of Hitchcock, and Jacob's Tavern, at the bottom of the footbridge, was a favorite of those living on The Knoll. It was not unusual to see women sitting at a bar smoking, drinking, and holding the attention of a crowd. At least it wasn't unusual for Ma. I could always tell what condition she was in when she was coming up the stairs at night, after spending time at the tavern because the odor hit my senses before she appeared at the door.

She would never be called a homemaker. If we needed a shirt hemmed or a button replaced, she would send us to Granny's. As far as cooking went, on a scale of one to ten, her homemaking skills would fall somewhere in the minus column. Her favorite menu consisted of Franco-American spaghetti out of a can, and fried veal loaf from the deli counter. Not exactly what you would call a gourmet delight. She would sometimes fill a five-quart pot with water, add ground beef along with salt and pepper, and bring it to a boil, before she added peeled and cut potatoes. When the grease rose to the top and formed a film, she announced supper was ready. It was always quite difficult getting through that meal.

Probably the tastiest meal she made was called Ala Crosby. Crosby was the last name of Dad's married sister. She gave Ma the recipe. It consisted of sliced potatoes and hamburger rolled into small meatballs. I think she added a bouillon cube to the meat and potatoes as she cooked them in the frying pan.

She did love to shop. I would have to give her a ten in that column. You would never hear me complain when she used those talents to add to the hangers in my closet.

The only other area she seemed to excel at was the annual activities and committee responsibilities of the church. She and her girlfriends spent several hours each month working on one project or another.

Dad was home in the evenings when we were younger, but as we got older, he found it necessary to add to the household income. His day job at the Springfield Armory, making M14 rifles, ended by three in the afternoon, and that meant he could work part time in the neighborhood package store one or two nights a week. Sometimes on Saturdays, he would wallpaper an apartment for someone in the parish and earn a few dollars. On occasion, I got to help him. I loved the smell of that wallpaper paste. Before long I got pretty good at the measuring and cutting tools he used on those job, if I do say so, myself.

Both of my parents found getting involved with the church, a satisfying outlet. Soon after the rectory was occupied by the new priest, Ma's involvement seemed to intensify.

Within weeks after his arrival, Father Fitz became a regular visitor at our house. Several nights each week, after supper he would come over, take off his white collar, hang up his black shirt and vest, put on one of my dad's shirts and they would all sit down in the parlor and have a few highballs. My father began to think of Father Fitz as one of his own brothers. He didn't even seem to mind that he smoked those big cigars. I would hear them discussing one event or another being planned by the parish that fell under one of my parent's organizations. If Dad had to work, the conversation would evolve around an event the women of the parish were planning.

The yearly minstrel shows, with men in black faces, was one of their annual events. They would now be moderated by Father Fitz and fell under the responsibilities of the men's Holy Name Society. That meant Dad had the ultimate lay-member-of-the-parish responsibility.

As soon as they wrapped up the final tallies on the minstrel, it was time to begin deciding on the theme they would use for the parish float in that year's St. Patrick's Day Parade. The Hitchcock parade drew marchers from as far away as California. Each year we prayed for good weather so the Mummers from Philadelphia could join us wearing those colorful feathers. The famous Kennedy's were regular marchers in our parade, whether they were in Boston or Washington, DC.

The same ten men of the parish would spend weeks building a float that would attract winning votes by the parade committee judges. Building props and completely covering the body of a truck took several weeks. The challenge to decide on a cleaver new theme each year, to ride down Main Street in front of the one carrying the Colleen and her Court, was under the direction of -you guessed it – Dad and Father Fitz.

When it came to the Women's Sodality, the active women of the church that Ma presided over, would not be outdone. Their annual fashion shows and card parties topped the competition's numbers. And whenever there was a month without a featured event, they would pull out the mimeograph machine, print hundreds of tickets, and hold a raffle.

With all the Catholic Churches in Hitchcock, you'd think taking turns from year to year would attract larger crowds and bring more financial support to the diocese. However, if you were Catholic in the fifties and sixties, your parish was the only game in town.

It was my first year on the executive committee of the Junior League of Mary. The previous year, as a freshman, I only attended their meetings and functions. At the end of the year, I was elected to the board of that respected assembly of high school girls and was looking forward to my new position with all the added responsibilities. An eagerness to do whatever it took to outshine the previous year's activities was my priority.

Father Fitz was the spiritual advisor to all three parish organizations and their activities. There was a lot to talk about in our parlor those nights. Still, he didn't stop at talking. At least, not where my mother was concerned.

CHAPTER THREE

It was the broken glass, all over the kitchen floor, that delayed me that Thursday night. Maureen and Norma were already at the meeting of the Junior League when I showed up, nearly a half hour late. Ma caused quite a scene at home that day. While I was used to her moods, that night she outdid herself.

My sister Connie and I were doing the dishes in the kitchen, and Ma was down the hall in her bedroom. In true sibling fashion, we were arguing over nothing. I guess we got loud enough to interrupt whatever she was doing. Before we knew it, she was at the sink, slapping us above our necks with movements hard enough to revive the unconscious.

Connie was drying a glass and held it up over her head in the dishtowel she had been using, in an effort to protect herself. Ma's hand came down hard enough to break the glass in several pieces. It's a good thing my sister had such kinky curly locks that it cushioned the space between the towel and her skull. I looked at Connie and cringed at the blood on her shirt. Ma backed off and ran into her bedroom.

I wasn't sure how to help Connie, or clean up all the aftermath, and it didn't appear that Ma was going to make that a teachable moment. So, I ran to the wall phone and called Dad who was working at Blanchard's, the neighborhood package store, at the end of our block. He came running down the street, took one look at us and hurried in to see Ma.

When he came back, he said, "She passes out at the sight of blood, and I wanted to make sure she was all right. Her hand needs stitches but she won't let me take her to a hospital."

Connie needed to have several pieces of glass removed from her hair and scalp. Most of them had shattered inside that dishtowel. She was quite a sight. Her curly afro-like blonde mane protected most of her scalp. Pulling glass from that tangled mess took forever.

Needless to say, the kitchen was sprinkled with glass droppings.

As the oldest of the siblings, I always drew the short straw. It was a miracle I was only a half hour late for the meeting of the Junior League. I was just grateful that no one mentioned the blotches on my face or the cuts on my hands.

Father Fitz was asking about the activities we were planning for the rest of the year. Everyone was talking at once, but you could hear the words "spring dance" repeatedly.

Finally, Father Fitz stood on top of his chair and raised a hand. When the room turned to silence, he went to the front desk and began.

"I think young women of this parish should be introduced into society and a spring dance would serve that purpose."

I personally thought he was confusing our mill town with Charleston, South Carolina. They had the cotillions. The girls in our school were used to standing on one side of the gymnasium while the boys stood on the other side. It usually took about two hours before anyone occupied the space in between. And then the nuns would say, "leave room for the Holy Ghost between your bodies young ladies," when we finally got asked to dance by a boy.

Back in the fifties we didn't really dance, we swayed. It was the only time we could wear our poodle skirts and those sweaters worn backwards with the attachable Peter Pan collars. The rest of the time we wore uniforms and we thought ours were the best Catholic high school uniforms in the city. The red and black plaid pleated skirts with white long-sleeved blouses and black vests made for a snappy appearance.

Beginning in my freshman year I would roll up my skirt at the waist, so it fell just above my knees.

About once a week Sister Ralph James would notice and call out, "Miss Newton, God doesn't want us to see your knees. Roll that skirt down immediately."

Father Fitz didn't think it was a problem at all. In fact, I think he liked it when we all raised our hemlines. Well, maybe not all of us, but certainly Jackie and Michelle. They were in the popular crowd and always sat in the front of the room. At most of these meetings they rested their legs on the tops of the desks in front of them.

By the end of the meeting, it was decided that this Spring Dance would be the Junior League of Mary's fundraiser for the year. Everyone was assigned to a different committee. For the next three months each girl at Saint Mary's High had some part in the preparation.

The students at the high school eventually accepted Father Fitz as one of those responsible for the daily happenings around the parish. Of course, they never called him Father Fitz. It was the accepted manner of the time to refer to everyone by his or her last name. So, they just called him Brennan. In the classroom, where he regularly taught Religion, they had to address him as Father, but behind his back he was just Brennan.

There was no greater respect shown to the nuns. Our mother superior, Sister Beatrice James, was called The Zombie by every student in the high school. The Sister part of all their names was always dropped. We would just say Ruth Marie, Bernadette Thomas, or whatever name they chose before their arrival at Saint Mary's.

As members of the Sisters of St. Joseph, they got to wear those overly starched white bibs on top of their long black dresses and the stiff white cardboard headpieces with their black veils made of the same fabric as the dress. It surrounded their heads and was probably the prototype for Sally Field's Flying Nun outfit in the sixties.

Their responsibilities covered more than just classroom teaching. It seemed like they were always just around the corner. They supervised after-school activities and stood out in the crowd at the special events we attended in the evening or on weekends. It was not unusual to see them up in the balcony at our monthly after school activities. In fact, it would be surprising if they weren't planted in the front row using their x-ray vision.

It was three weeks before the big fundraising dance. Ma and I were in the kitchen putting the sheets through the ringer. The weight of the fabric full of water from the washer always took the two of us to lift. As Ma would wind the handle to squeeze the water out, I would feed her more of the sheet from the washer's basin to put through the rollers.

"I'll be chaperoning the fundraising dance this year as part of my Sodality duties, and Dad has to work that night, so I'll need you to baby-sit," she said in the same tone she used when she asked me to pass the salt. I dropped my end of the sheet. Her body jerked as hot water splashed her left side.

"You do realize that the Junior League is in charge of that dance," I said probably faster than I intended. She was well aware of my role in the League that year. "What will everyone think, if I don't show up?"

Aside from the fact that Maureen, Norma, and I had been talking for weeks about what we would wear, I also had a responsibility to honor.

"I have no idea who else might be available that night, but tell you what. If you get all the ironing done before the dance, I'll see what I can do," she finally said just above a whisper. She looked straight ahead like she was talking to someone outside our kitchen window. I figured she was just thinking about whom she might ask to baby-sit.

Back then ironing was no simple task. We pressed everything made of fabric - hankies, sheets, and even underwear. We would sprinkle them with water, roll them up and put them in the refrigerator before they were ready for the iron. I was like a one-woman production line for the next three weeks. All I did was iron.

The day of the dance Ma informed me, "I wasn't able to get anyone else to watch your sisters, so you'll have to stay home tonight."

Every other sophomore girl in my school would be going. How could I face my classmates and the other members of the League when, as an officer, I didn't show up for the biggest event of the year? I was numb. It hurt to breathe.

I knew from experience, there was no talking to Ma. I felt like I was walking in a dream.

I'm not sure how I got through that Thursday night, or how I was able to go to school the next day. Everyone was whispering as I walked by. I would go around a corner and two more girls would straighten up when they saw me. I knew they were all talking about me. What could I say?

It was lunchtime before I ran into Maureen and Norma. It took a long time that morning to get rid of the red blotches around my eyes from crying. I just yelled out the window for them to go on to school without me. I noticed that they were acting strange, as well. They knew how my mother could be at times, so I was surprised they weren't more sympathetic. Our conversation even seemed strained.

By the end of classes, it was nearly impossible to get out of the building without the stares and giggles. As we came around the corner onto Beech Street, a group of my classmates started chiding me "Where were you last night when Brennan and your mother were parking at the dam?"

I froze when I heard those words. Could this really be happening, I wondered. I can still feel that strange emptiness in my body like it happened moments ago. They couldn't possibly be right.

Ma was always the center of attention at parties and family gatherings but kissing our parish priest…never.

I was sure Ma would have an explanation for what appeared on the surface to be an act of adultery. I was also certain that we would all laugh about this egregious misunderstanding when Father Fitz came over that night.

I wanted to run home and ask Ma directly, but the words sounded crazy as I practiced saying them on my way from class. I surely didn't want to get her upset enough to put her in one of her moods. I would just wait until after supper, when the dishes were all cleared and put away, and the adults were settled into their regular routine of drinking and talking and talking and drinking.

Yet, no one came to our front door that night. In fact, three nights went by without the smell of that cigar wafting through the parlor air. I didn't know what to do.

When we returned to school on Monday, my friends never mentioned the dance or what they saw afterward, but I couldn't stop thinking about their accusation.

I thought about going to talk to Granny, but how could I tell her there was a possibility that her daughter-in-law could be cheating on her son. And with a Catholic priest to boot.

On the fourth night, the doorbell rang and there he was, taking off his collar, putting on one of Dad's shirts and moving on into the parlor. The three of them got into their routine as always. Dad was just as talkative and friendly as ever. I tried to see if Ma acted any different when she spoke to the man she was supposed to have kissed.

If there was something going on between Ma and Father Fitz, they were good at concealing it. So good, it made me wonder, who was this woman I called Ma?

CHAPTER FOUR

Ma could drink any of my uncles under the table. Agatha Margaret Sheehan grew up with a reputation as a party girl. When she married my dad, the Newton family counted on her to be the life of all their parties. She didn't disappoint.

With her curly dark hair and white freckled face, she screamed Irish, and looked like the Aggie they all called her. She always came up with the best costumes for the family's Halloween gatherings, held the attention of the largest crowds and she was known to smoke like a wet bonfire.

I never knew how my parents met. I always assumed they knew each other from the neighborhood. They never discussed their courtship or any other part of their single lives.

It wasn't until after Ma's death that I found out she was in the same class in school as Dad's sister, Marie.

They were two years younger than Dad.

I don't remember Grandma Sheehan, even though there was a picture on the parlor table of her holding me in her lap when I was a toddler. Maybe my memories of her are vague because I was only two years old when she died.

There was never any mention of Ma's father, except that he was dead, and there were no pictures of him anywhere. At some point during my teenage years, I heard he fell down the stairs to his death.

Even Ma and Dad's wedding pictures didn't have any other family except Dad's brother George, who served as Dad's best man, and Ma's friend, Gertrude, who served as her Maid of Honor.

There were occasional visits to one of Ma's aunt's during my younger years. We called her Maggie. It really never became a question for us growing up to ask about Ma's family. We just accepted her silence as fact.

Dad was in the Army by the time I was born, and when I was two years old, he was sent to Aberdeen Proving Ground in Maryland. Ma stayed in Hitchcock, but according to Granny, she hated being tied to the house.

Years later, when I was pregnant with my first daughter, Granny told me that when Dad was stationed in

Maryland, she went to our apartment one day to visit us and found me crying in my crib. Ma wasn't around and didn't answer her frantic calls, so she took me back to her apartment. There was never any talk about the incident, even years later. I know that Granny was never a big fan of Ma's. It was the forties. People didn't talk about their feelings. Sort of how there was never any mention of Cancer. People would just refer to it as the Big C.

Our backyard faced Granny's apartment across the alley, and the milkman, iceman, and ragman would drive through on a regular basis selling and delivering their goods. "Rags for sale" was a weekly sonnet heard throughout the neighborhood.

The first apartment we lived in was on the fifth floor of a brick tenement on Beech Street. Our backyards were similar with all our porches painted gray. There were days when we would all run down to the vegetable wagon when Mr. Joe drove through. "Give me the freshest corn you've got," was a regular request.

The large blocks of ice would be carried up the back stairs each week with huge tongs and put in our iceboxes. It was never clear what time the milkman left the bottles at our back door. I just remember opening the door during the winter months. Making sure the cream on the top didn't freeze and push that cardboard lid far enough up the bottle to cause a mess, was a constant challenge.

There was a small grocery store in the alley where we would go often to buy staples and put them on the charge account. The owners knew everyone and became like family to most of the local households. Daily shopping was the preferred method back then, at least in our neighborhood. "What'll you have today Mrs. Newton," the clerk would ask.

It was during the time Dad was away that I was exposed to the first of Ma's many secrets. We were walking down the back-porch stairs on our way to the store, when this little yippy dog came jumping at us. Ma let out a scream, held my hands up high, and placed me in front of her. There were only inches between me and the dog. He didn't have to jump very high to reach the middle of a three-year-old body. He bit my stomach. Ma was more than afraid. She was petrified. She shook for hours after I stopped crying. There was very little blood, but the event caused my lifetime internal scar.

After our encounter with little yippy, she would avoid being anywhere near a dog. It's not surprising that I also had that fear. Growing up and spending time with my grandparents at their camp exposed me to their old dog Charlie. I'm not sure if it was because he was not little and yippy, or just because Granny made it seem like he was just part of the family, but I never felt afraid of him. As for dogs in general, it was years before I could stay on the same side of the street when I saw one coming. Walking back from school or the drugstore, or just about anywhere else, I would go inside a hallway and peek through the door until the dog passed. It got so bad that when I started dating in high school I even jumped up on the back of my date when one came prancing down the street.

Years later when my daughters wanted a dog of their own, I spent at least four weeks visiting the local pet store until I was able to pick up the puppy that blended in with my rabbit fur coat. After multiple trips just to hold the Lhasa Apso, I was able to bring him home without the need of a tranquilizer and a step stool to keep me off the ground while he ran around like puppies usually do before they settle into their eating and sleeping routine. The task forced me to use an inner strength I never knew I had.

Ma's fear of dogs was just one of the many secrets she kept to herself. After that day on the back-porch stairs, she would tell everyone that I was the one afraid and she would have to leave anywhere there was a dog, so I didn't get scared. She was so convincing even I believed her.

She was also afraid of the water. I never saw her swim. She would tell us not to go above our waists because we might drown. I guess she felt limiting us to waist-high water was her safety net. I think she tried. At least, I thought she did. I realized later that I didn't know what normal was. Just because it was normal for me, was it really normal? Or was I living in a world of my own?

With the introduction to water and swimming that I received, it's not surprising that I was taking swimming lessons in the town pool with five-year-old's when I was in the eighth grade. It took months to pass that test. Even then, I think it was because all of the instructors felt sorry for me. I never did swim well enough to pass. I just convinced the lifeguard that I would be able to save myself with the sidestroke. That way I could keep my head out of the water.

Years later, when I moved to San Diego with my two young daughters, most of the suburban houses had pools in their backyards. I thought I should really try to learn how to swim in case one of the girls fell in. I was surprised to learn that several of my California neighbors needed lessons as well. We found an instructor at San Diego State University who looked just like Burt Bacharach's younger brother and decided we would do anything for him. Even put our faces in the water. The only thing I learned for sure was that my children would learn to swim as soon as they could walk.

Right after my sister Connie was born, Ma seemed to get nervous about most everything. Even at five years old I noticed her hand shaking when she put a cigarette in her mouth and held it there until she drew enough nicotine to blow out a long trail of gray smoke.

It became common for her to call on neighbors and friends to calm her nerves and talk through her upsetting situations. She did have more responsibility and another mouth to feed, but everything just seemed tougher for Ma.

Medical concerns seemed to make her exceptionally nervous. When any of us got a fever, she would begin to panic.

I can still remember the time when Ma sat at the table in the kitchen with Granny and Mrs. McKenna from next door. I had been in my bed with a fever for four days.

I could hear lots of talking because my bedroom was right off the kitchen. When I finally opened the door one afternoon, they all started crying. They didn't think I would be able to walk. They were afraid that the Polio virus I was fighting would cripple me for life. Lots of people during that time ended up in iron lungs. A little uneven step from time to time was all I was left with, mostly when the weather is damp. If you didn't know, you would never suspect.

By the time Hannah was born, Ma seemed nervous all the time. She would be silent for hours and her smoking increased. My sisters and I have memories of being told that Hannah was a twin, but there were never any details from Ma or anything beyond the stated fact. We just assumed the other baby died at birth. Maybe that was why she seemed so nervous.

It was common for her to send me to the store when she needed a new pack of cigarettes. There was no legal age requirement in Massachusetts at the time for purchasing such items and we had an account at the store. By the age of eight or nine, I would go to the store, pick up the necessities, walk up to the counter and say, "Ma wants these, and a pack of Winston's and she said to put it on the bill, please."

Most summers during my single digit years, Ma sent me to my grandparents' camp about forty-five minutes east of The Knoll. That's where I felt most at home. I loved spending time with Granny and Grandpa.

The camp sat up the hill from a pond in the country with a real outhouse on the property. People still used that outhouse even after there was one inside the camp. A full set of stairs took you down from the camp to the dressing rooms - one for the females and a separate one for the males - on a landing halfway down to the pond. When all the aunts, uncles and cousins arrived on weekends, the two front lawns would be covered with bodies. The kids would congregate on one lawn and the adults on the other. They became the regular gathering places for the whole family.

All the women would cook in the outdoor building they called the summer kitchen. You could see the steam rising out of the open window as the corn was boiling in pots inside. Sometimes it would encompass the glider swings my cousins and I regularly played on, between the summer kitchen and the kids' lawn.

Because I was the oldest of the grandchildren, which would eventually number twenty-six, they pulled out all the stops for my fifth birthday party. My aunt Sarah, nearly ten years my senior, and the youngest of my aunts, was usually in charge of the decorations for such occasions. She placed long picnic tables side by side with party-like coverings and balloons tied to the place settings. It wasn't hard to feel special with all that fuss, not to mention the sheer numbers of people in attendance bearing presents for the birthday girl.

Uncle Harry was my Godfather, and he always gave me the best presents. I don't remember what my parents gave me for any of my birthdays or special events - not even for my high school graduation. But Uncle Harry gave me a gray Samsonite suitcase that day with a shiny clasp and handle strap. It's funny what one remembers from childhood. Maybe it was because he was single for most of my younger years and was able to spend more on gifts. Or maybe I just felt like he took extra care when he shopped for me.

When everyone would leave camp on Sunday evenings I would sit on the screened in porch with Granny and play Scat. We would each get three cards and would have to put up three nickels for each game. I think she let me win more nickels playing that card game than I deserved. I always felt special with Granny.

One summer when she and Grandpa were packing up the car to go out to camp there was great drama in the backyard. I was rushing to get my things into the back seat of the car and wasn't paying attention to the fact that I had my hand on the door jamb until Grandpa flipped the door closed and caught my middle finger at the knuckle. There was a lot of pain and tears and I think Granny took several years to get over her guilt. I'm not sure why she felt so guilty; it was Grandpa who slammed the door.

I never had many friends over the house during my formative years, or any year for that matter. I didn't realize then that there was anything wrong with that picture. I thought it was because I just wanted to go to friends' houses instead. But, come to think of it, I didn't really do much of that either.

Out of the house was the place where I interacted with my peers. There was the regular pick-up game of Double Dutch with the rest of the jump-roping crowd in the schoolyard after class, and there were other times when we tried to perfect our skills with "Jacks."

We made things from objects we found and pretended they were something else. Our imaginations were always working and coming up with something new to keep us busy until we would get called in at bedtime. During the summer months the streets of The Knoll always came alive after dark. We could hear families arguing with one another or mothers calling their children home with "this is the last time before I come out there," warning. And there was always a smell of someone cooking a late supper. If it was a Friday, the aroma of fish and chips from the Busy Bee could be inhaled throughout the six-block neighborhood. Saturday nights were a favorite of mine because we always brought home those fresh baked beans and brown bread from the bakery on the corner of Elm and Beech.

It seemed like, for as far back as I can remember, I did a lot of babysitting and chores around the house. Taking the clothes in off the line was one of my regular jobs. On colder days the sheets would be frozen and took time bending them into position. Making sure the wooden clothespins were placed in the cloth bag Ma hung from the lines was a required step in the chore, even before folding or rolling the clothes to be ironed.

Some memories are more vivid than others. Like that summer afternoon before I turned eleven. Connie was six.

We had left the fifth-floor walkup by then and moved across the street to the first floor of a two-family house. We were hanging out in our grassy fenced-in backyard when Ma yelled out that she was busy, and I was to listen for Hannah who was napping because she didn't feel well. We got into one of our "playing school" routines where I was always the teacher and Connie was my only pupil. I loved correcting her papers, but never imagined that it would be a thirty-year practice later in life.

After a while, the next-door neighbor came out on her porch and called down to us. She lived in the second-floor tenement apartment and would ask me to watch her six-year-old daughter while she went grocery shopping each week. For that I earned a dollar.

She had just brought home a new kitten and invited us up to hold the cuddly ball of fur. We were only up there a few minutes when we heard Ma's blood-curdling screams. We hurried out to the edge of the porch and realized she couldn't find Hannah.

Soon several of the neighbors were out on the street to offer their help. They called Hannah's name and even though it seemed like hours, a few minutes later she was discovered across the street in the tenement where my aunt lived. The woman on the first floor took Hannah inside her apartment when she heard her in the hallway calling for my aunt upstairs.

Ma was furious. She dragged us back to our house, got out my father's belt and hit me on my back until it was wet. After all, I was supposed to be listening for Hannah. That brown belt of Dad's was a familiar discipline tool for Ma. She would sometimes say, "Wait until your father gets home." And we would think, "Oh please, let's wait." He was definitely not the one who frequented the brown belt.

It was common during those years for discipline to include spanking or some other form of physical discipline. Dad preferred to use the phrase "Do you want me to stop this car?"

It wasn't until years later when I was in therapy that the question of, "where was Ma that afternoon" came up. So many other questions arose as well. But I'm getting ahead of myself.

On Friday nights, during the fifties, we all went to Granny's to watch the Gillette Cavalcade of Sports. She was one of the first to buy a television in the neighborhood and we thought it was a special treat to sit in a semi-circle on the floor of her parlor, eating candy dots from long strips of paper, eager to see what that big square box with short legs would show us.

Ma always had a story or joke to get my aunts and uncles laughing. It was strange to see her so calm when she was out in large crowds. Maybe because there was always alcohol involved. We looked forward to our time with family and couldn't wait for the next week's television special. *Henry Aldrich* and *I Remember Mama* were two of my favorites.

Some of my fondest memories are from the times in Granny and Grandpa's parlor. Any time there was an occasion to celebrate, it happened in that room.

Christmas Eve was extra special. We would join all of my cousins gathered there to wait for an appearance from Santa Claus before he began his rounds on his sleigh.

We all dressed in our finest attire and most of the granddaughters arrived sporting our newly cut Mamie Eisenhower bangs. My aunt Marie always made her three daughters matching dresses.

We couldn't wait to see if Grandpa added new houses, or people in his village, under the Christmas tree. He had colored lights in the cardboard houses and set them up on pretend streets. There was even a pair of skaters on top of a mirror surrounded by lots of cotton. We thought of it as our very own visit to winter wonderland.

I loved sitting on the floor between Grandpa's village and the cardboard fireplace he put up each year for the holiday. But, after the year my cousin announced to everyone that Santa was wearing the same shoes as my uncle David, the sleigh no longer stopped at Granny's on the night before Christmas.

Christmas presents were Ma's specialty. She came from a poor family and wanted her daughters to have the nicest gifts they could afford, even if Dad did have to work three jobs to cover the costs.

My cousins were not happy the year the three of them got walking dolls and brought them to Granny's on Christmas day, only to see me and my sisters arriving with our three walking dolls that were at least six inches taller.

Ma always bought the best name brands she could afford and hid them in our closets, so Dad didn't see them. She did the same with her own clothes. Then when she wore a new dress and Dad asked if it was new, she would say, "oh no, I've had this for a while." I guess that's where she got the idea to include the booze in the closets with all the other packages in later years.

Her biggest pet peeve was with the monthly requests from the Nuns during our elementary years. On the last Friday of the month, we had to bring in a pair of our fathers' old socks and put them on over our shoes to slide around and buff the hardwood floors in our classrooms.

Some kids brought in empty Wonder Bread bags until their fathers wore enough holes in his socks to give them up. Ma said that the janitors were getting enough money to take care of the floors. I think the Nuns felt it was their way of keeping us in line and showing us who was boss.

My room in our Beech Street house was off the kitchen and under the back stairs that led up to the landlord's apartment on the second floor. It was a little dark, but it was all mine. I didn't have to share a room like my sisters. My window looked out to the back of the funeral home next door. The window across from mine looked into their embalming area where they took dead people to get prepared for the coffin and viewing. After observing men working on a dead body one night, who suddenly sat upright, my blinds stayed closed until the day we moved to our very own house in the next town. Maybe that was why I always thought it was dark in my room.

Ma never took me to any of my medical or dental

appointments. She didn't like doctors or hospitals. She even seemed afraid to be near anything connected with the medical profession. She put Dad in charge of our health issues. It became routine for me to go to the dentist at the bottom of Main Street with him. The elevator operator would close those wrought iron doors and drive the elevator to the top floor dentist's office. He was the one man I hated to see.

There was a time when he just pulled a tooth out of my mouth without using Novocain. I remember screaming and being held down. From that day forward I would avoid going to see him at all costs.

But, when I developed a mouthful of abscessed teeth in the eighth grade, I had to follow a regiment of weekly treatments to fix the problem. Ma would never want to go with me, so she convinced me I was old enough to go by myself. I remember walking over the footbridge and downtown for those weekly appointments and thinking of ways to get out of actually getting on that elevator.

Winters on The Knoll brought out the hoses so the field at the Maple Street Public School could get flooded for ice-skating. During those times we would meet kids from the other part of The Knoll who didn't go to Catholic schools.

The Carvers were the only black family I knew from the Knoll. They had twenty-seven children and were famous because they all lived in one tenement on the street behind the public school.

Segregation was not a part of our lives. We never even discussed it. The problems experienced elsewhere didn't make it into the discussions at our supper tables. Even though the Supreme Court ruling in 1954 declared segregation in public schools was unconstitutional, it changed nothing in my life. We never even heard the story of Rosa Parks or any stories of the problems in our own state of Massachusetts. The many segregation problems experienced by the residents of South Boston and Charlestown, two hours east of us, didn't really come into fruition until the seventies. I guess you could say we grew up in our own little bubble.

Our summers always included a week or two at either Hampton Beach in New Hampshire or Misquamicut Beach in Rhode Island. It seemed like everyone from The Knoll just picked up their belongings and moved closer to the ocean for as long as they could afford to be away. That summer after Father Fitz arrived in Hitchcock, he joined our family at the beach. My sister Hannah only remembers how she had to wait each morning to get to enjoy the waves in the ocean until Father Fitz finished saying his morning prayers.

By then most of the people in the neighborhood knew about Ma's relationship with Father Fitz. It was only my father and sisters who seemed to have no knowledge of the affair. I didn't know what to do about it. I didn't want to be the one to tell Dad.

Ma was afraid I might try to tell him, so she spent her days looking for ways to prove that I was not to be trusted just in case I did try to expose her dirty little secret. We never talked about her affair, but she knew I knew. I noticed that she appeared more nervous and had a lot more meetings in the evening. My closet was getting crowded with bottles of alcohol.

It was the summer of my fifteenth year that I finally got my period. All of my friends had already experienced the monthly arrival. My experience was not like anything they passed on to me in our after-school conversations. I actually doubled over in pain the afternoon it arrived, and I was sure there would be a trip to the hospital because of the blood that landed on our bathroom floor. When I called

Ma to come to my aid she just said, "It's to be expected, wait here," and she left the room.

When she returned a few minutes later she had an old facecloth in her hand and something she called a sanitary belt. It wrapped around your waist and had strips of elastic with hooks coming down in front and back. Ma said, "hook this in your underpants and make sure to change it every day until the bleeding stops." There were other cloths like it in a special place that only she and I could use. She made sure there were always clean cloths there for us. About six months later she began purchasing sanitary napkins. They replaced the cloths and made things a lot more manageable. They were disposable.

In a matter of less than an hour after the bleeding began, I vomited and continued for the next twelve hours until the dry heaves wore me out and I fell asleep. This became a pattern that interrupted my normal routine every month for many years after that day of passage.

There was never any "birds and bees" conversation with Ma. Any knowledge I had, came from the girls in my class. Since I was one of the last girls in my neighborhood to receive what some referred to as "the curse," it probably wasn't necessary to discuss much with her. In my circle, it was called "my friend."

I had full knowledge about what happened in the mating game. It was enhanced with my nightly chapter of Peyton Place.

Ma was busy starring in her own romance novel. Just not one I wanted to read.

CHAPTER FIVE

Bobby Darin's, *Mack the Knife*, was number one on the charts that summer. It was the one between my sophomore and junior year of high school. I started spending more nights with my friends in the park at the end of our street, and Bobby's voice could be heard each night coming from the radios in the cars lining the streets.

Ma and Father Fitz were busy doing whatever adults did when they were trying to keep their relationship a secret from the rest of the world. It was hard for me to believe that they didn't know just how many people were aware of what they were doing. Then again, maybe they did and didn't care.

Some nights I had to be home by nine so Ma could go out. Dad was working and Connie was only ten years old. Certainly not old enough to be in charge of her eight-year-old sister.

That summer was when I really began to hate Ma. There was no reason why I should have to give up my time with my friends as a high school student in my coming-out years, so my mother could cheat on my father with our parish priest. I came very close to telling Dad that summer. The only thing that stopped me was the chain of events that began in the park.

It started with the competitive games we all played for nickels. Jackknife was our game of choice. We could spend hours playing the game with as many participants as the park could hold. We all had jackknives and became experts on all the moves. My best moves were off my left knee. I won enough money during the month of June to buy myself a new bathing suit. Maybe I could just take out my frustration with what was going on at home by becoming the best at this nightly competition.

By July, the activity drew kids from other parts of Hitchcock. I became friendly with a girl from Morrisville who was dating a boy from our neighborhood. She kept asking me to double date with her and her boyfriend's best friend.

I only had one date before that. It was up at Hampton Beach the previous summer. The boy in the next room at the motel was from upstate New York and was a year older than me. He took me to the Wednesday night fireworks on the beach. We stayed on the sand after the festivities, and I got my second kiss.

My first one came as a surprise the previous spring. After choir practice, a bunch of us in the junior choir hung out for hours on Duncan Street and played Truth, Dare, Consequences, Promise or Repeat. On a dare I kissed Jimmy Durgin in the hallway across from the church. Most of my friends wanted to kiss him and were jealous I got the question that forced the issue. He didn't know it was my first. At least, I don't think he knew.

Going on a double date was nothing like I had imagined. Dating was never on my radar. Anytime I thought about it my mind would wander to scenes of Ma with Father Fitz. It made me shiver all over.

There were other kids dating from our crowd. They were the ones who always stayed on the park benches cuddling after our games ended. Anyone with a car just left and headed for the dam where all the parkers frequented.

Eventually my friends wore me down and I agreed to go on a double date with Mike Moriarty. My girlfriends had to come to my house and literally get me dressed.

I found out later that Mike's friends had to get him out of a tree to agree to the date - so much for the proper start of a lasting relationship. It would have had more potential for success if at least one party wanted to spend time with the other. Mike's best friend, Johnny picked up his girlfriend in Morrisville and after they got Mike, the three of them stopped for me on our way to the Eastern States Exposition – or as we called it - the Big E. The ride from The Knoll down Riverdale Road took about forty minutes and by the time we arrived, I learned that we were both pretty new at the dating game. I was determined to just relax and enjoy the evening.

It was the first time I was in the back seat of a car on a date. Actually, it was my first real date.

Ma didn't seem to have any objection when I said I was going. She knew I probably would not stay quiet about her nighttime activities if she didn't let me go on that date.

Mike was a year ahead of me in school, about to start his senior year. His backyard faced mine with an ally in between. A few years earlier, he was out there chasing the boy who lived upstairs from us and threw a rock that accidentally hit me in the neck which left me with a small scar. The only thing I knew about him - other than his rock throwing capabilities - was that he was considered to be one of the smartest kids in his class.

The Big E was, and still is, like a huge county fair. It covers all the New England States and is held each year on the fairgrounds in West Springfield. There is a different building for each state that holds products and merchandise made locally. There were potatoes in the Maine building and maple syrup in the one from Vermont and so on. You could watch agricultural competitions, spend hours, and get dizzy on amusement rides, and play games that afforded you an opportunity to win stuffed animals. There was more food than anyone could eat during a week's worth of attendance. The odors of French fries and fried sugar and cinnamon doughnuts grabbed me at each turn.

Mike was pretty quiet that night. We went on several rides, checked out the States buildings and tried our luck at several games before he won and presented me with a pink bunny.

By the time we got back to the neighborhood I had my third kiss. Best of all, I now had other things on my mind and Ma's affair would just have to run its' course.

When school started that fall, we began a new routine. I started seeing more of Mike after school and on weekends. On Saturday nights soon after Mike passed his driving test, we would ride down the Riverdale Road to the latest teenage hangout - the A&W Root Beer Drive-In. The waiters rode out to our cars on roller skates to serve us our food. I couldn't get enough of that orange soda and their chilidogs were, hands down, the best ones around.

One Saturday night we went to a movie and then drove down to the dam in his father's car with all the other student parkers. I was nervous that I might run into Ma in one of the cars parked along the waters' edge.

Today I would consider the activity going on at the dam back then to be Hitchcock's version of the preparation for entrance into the Mile-High Club.

But we never made it to the start of the line of cars because Mike bumped into another car in front of us that stopped suddenly right after we turned off the main road. The front bumper on our car hooked over the back bumper on the car in front like two pieces of Lego's and no matter how many times the guys jumped on the tangled mess they could not separate the two cars. Mike only had his license a few months and was sure his parents would be furious. There was no escaping the call to his father to come and help him break the car loose. We didn't want his parents to know that we were on our way to go parking, so I left the area with the girl in the other car and walked the six blocks home to The Knoll.

Months later we learned that Mike's father worried that there were no girls with the cars and wondered why he was there with the other guy. I'm sure he was relieved to find out I had left. Gays were not accepted in the fifties. In fact, they weren't even mentioned. It would have been considered a mortal sin to be in a relationship with someone of the same sex.

Even though I saw much less of Ma during that fall, her affair was still going strong. The visits from Father Fitz continued, but I was hardly home to watch the charade. Besides, most of their contact happened elsewhere.

My membership in the Junior League of Mary required my attendance at regular meetings, but other than that I avoided seeing Father Fitz outside of the normal high school activities.

About that time, I began having trouble sleeping and seemed to be getting nervous all the time myself. Maybe it was something in our drinking water. On several Sunday mornings I felt faint while kneeling in the church pew during Mass. When I went to see our family doctor for a routine checkup, she prescribed a mild tranquilizer.

She knew about Ma's affair and felt my nerves were caused from the stress of keeping the secret from Dad.

That spring Dad bought a new red Dodge Coronet Lancer for nearly two thousand dollars. It had tail fins that made it look like it would fly. A month later Ma got her license. I was excited because I would soon be old enough to get a license of my own.

I found out quickly that was a non-starter. They wouldn't teach me how to drive a car at sixteen. Ma hadn't driven on her own long enough to be able to teach someone else and Dad felt I was too young to be driving a car at all.

I really think Ma was afraid I would follow her and Father Fitz if I had a license. Or maybe I would want to use the car and she wouldn't be able to go out at night. Whatever the reason, there were no lessons for me.

Around November, Ma took a job at our local hangout - The Attic. There was a small group of neighbors who would stop in for a hamburger or cup of coffee, but it was mostly occupied by high school students after school and in the evenings. We would hang out, drink vanilla cokes, and talk about everything we couldn't discuss in front of the nuns.

Playing the jukebox was the first thing we did when we arrived. My favorite was *You Are My Destiny* by Paul Anka. I played that number twenty-six over and over until I ran out of money.

Two of the boys in our class always seemed to be the ones to entertain the crowd. Joey had a glass eye and took it out and rolled it on the table in one of the booths as often as he could get a laugh, and Jack just kept us laughing regularly. Sometimes it was hard to control him even in school.

Sister Bernadette Roberts loved plants and had them growing in pots on the windowsills along the back of her classroom. She also had a problem with her eyesight. It was failing. It allowed for the boys in the class to sit in the back rows, crack open the windows and smoke cigarettes. One day Jack threw his match in the potted plant and the plant caught on fire. A few minutes later we heard Sister in the front of the room, "Get down on your knees, children. It's another burning bush." We repeated those words to one another for at least a year and laughed out loud each time.

I always wondered what kind of education the nuns got before they came into our classrooms. They often tried to encourage the girls in the class to enter the novitiate and become nuns. We never thought of the novitiate as a college, so we didn't think they had much schooling beyond high school before they arrived in our classrooms to teach.

They seemed more intent on selling raffle tickets for the fundraisers to support the church. When Sister Bernard Francis asked me what I thought I should get for my final grade in biology that year, I said an A. "Why do you think you deserve an A, Miss Newton," she asked? "Because you pushed us into that competition and I sold the most raffle tickets this year," I replied. I got an A for the course. I'm not sure I passed the biology final.

There were two paths one could follow at St. Mary's High. There was the classical track for those students who knew they wanted to go on to college, and there was the commercial track for the rest of us.

Dad didn't have the money for me to go to college and besides in the late fifties' girls were not encouraged to go to college unless you had your heart set on nursing or teaching. If not, you prepared to be nuns or secretaries. I had no desire to spend each day in that stiff white headdress and bib. I followed the commercial track.

Typing on those manual Underwood typewriters and scribbling those characters in steno pads had become part of my daily routine.

These career choices were just stopgaps toward the real lifestyle everyone felt girls needed to prepare for – the one called housewife and mother. Our high school didn't offer gym classes or home economics. We were on our own when it came to cooking or working off the calories we put on from our favorite recipes.

We did offer religion classes. Scratch that. We required religion classes. Father Fitz taught Religion one through four. There was no escaping a class with him.

Mike completed his senior year and graduated that June. He was the salutatorian of his class. As a junior, I was one of the ushers that guided the families to their pews in the church for the graduation ceremony. They called us the honor guards.

Naturally, it was held in the upstairs church with a Solemn High Mass as part of the ceremony. The Nuns would lead each of the high school classes up the side outside aisles of the church in order of rank, and sit with them during the awarding of diplomas.

When the choir began the ceremony with their rendi-

-tion of *St. Mary's Bells*, the student ushers led the graduates into the church and stood at the entrance to each pew as the graduates filed into their rows for the beginning of the Mass and the awarding of their degrees.

This was the time each year that the student body tried to sing louder than the choir during the chorus. Their version was different. At the top of their lungs, they sang *St. Mary's smells*. Inevitably during that opening song, Zombie, our Mother Superior, would walk up to the loudest singers and give them that look that could turn the worst of them into stone.

When the ceremony ended the graduates led everyone out of the church to the choir's most loved tradition of *The Song of Praise*.

The party afterwards was held at Mike's new house on Hadley Street in the valley. As the first of his three siblings to graduate from high school, and the first of the Moriarty family to attend college, there was extra special partying going on in that house. I think they were more excited that he got accepted into the electrical engineering program at University of Massachusetts than he was.

By this time, I was a regular at their family gatherings. It was such a different feeling than what I was used to at my house. Mike's mother was a great cook and an even better baker. She made an apple pie to die for. But she was famous for her mincemeat squares dusted with powdered sugar.

That summer before he went away to college, we spent our days working and our nights close. Mike worked at the tobacco farms in Connecticut along with nearly twenty other guys from Hitchcock. A truck would show up on the corner early each morning and take a bunch of the guys to the farms and deliver them back at night.

I got a job downtown on the corner of Winter and Speen in the Tuberculosis and Health Association office. It was mostly filing health records and helping out at vaccination clinics in the city. But they also operated a treatment facility at a former day camp on the hills to the west of the city. It was the first municipal sanatorium just outside of Boston and was able to house twenty-eight patients at full capacity.

That summer Granny and Grandpa let the nuns use the camp for a long weekend. Mike and I thought it would be fun to notify our friends and classmates of the outing. We could check out what the nuns wore under those confining outfits. It wasn't surprising to learn that most of them had full heads of hair. It was the one that had bright red that kept us talking for the rest of the summer. Her eyebrows never gave her away. Were nuns allowed to use dye?

Most weekends anyone with a car from The Knoll headed for the beach. My girlfriend, Molly, and I decided we would do something to surprise our boyfriends for the Fourth-of-July beach excursion. Her mother had a sewing machine and we wanted to make them Bermuda shorts.

We had no idea we were choosing to start with an article of clothing that an advanced seamstress would avoid. We went to the fabric store downtown and bought a pattern. Not being able to find one for Bermuda shorts, we chose one for boxer shorts. We would just make the legs longer.

It took several days of non-stop foot peddling before we got to the hardest part. There seemed to be all this extra fabric in the front of the shorts. We couldn't imagine they would need all that. The pattern had to be wrong. So, we just cut it away and put in a zipper. That process took extra time because there was no zipper in the boxer shorts package. We just improvised.

The day of the trip, we couldn't wait for the guys to open their surprise presents. We parked the car behind the

Casino and spent the day on the beach. The regular routine would include pouring the baby oil with iodine on each other to take full advantage of the saltwater and sun on our bodies. Skin cancer was yet to be feared.

By the end of the afternoon, we were ready to shower in the bathhouse and put on our walking-on-the-boardwalk evening clothes. That's when we made them open our presents and told them to exchange them for whatever they had planned to wear that night.

I must say they were good sports. Probably because we had been talking about the project for weeks.

When they met us back at the bandstand, we didn't realize at first that they both were wearing their polo shirts outside their shorts. But it didn't take long for us to understand why. It's surprising their voices didn't get any higher.

The fabric we had cut off was really needed to allow for the room required in that area of their body. The zippers nearly castrated them on contact. They walked bent over to avoid any unnecessary contact with the zipper. We put them out of their misery about twenty steps toward the restaurant. They went to change.

We naturally wanted to act like it would be a piece of

cake to correct the problem for the next trip to the beach. But they never saw those shorts again and it would be years before I ever attempted to put fabric to a sewing machine.

In late August, Mike's parents drove him up to Amherst for his first semester at UMASS. I couldn't imagine how I would get through the days until he came home for Thanksgiving. I wasn't looking forward to going back to school for my senior year.

I had been elected President of the Junior League of Mary and would be working with Father Fitz on a regular basis. I avoided any interaction with him or Ma over the summer and had no idea what to expect to find at home. Things hadn't changed much. Just more of their evening routine with drinks in our parlor. It was very obvious that Dad still had no idea what went on when he wasn't there. Could Dad really be that blind? Was it my imagination or was Ma gaining weight?

CHAPTER SIX

Learning to live without my lifeline only made me stronger. For the first time in months, I didn't have Mike to hang out with. I needed to find ways to stay away from places that would remind me of the affair going on under my nose.

My senior year was busy with school activities and answering Mike's weekly letters. Engineering classes were far from the classes he mastered at St. Mary's. For the first time in his life, he faced the possibility of a failing grade. It made for a lot more studying on his part. Needless to say, there was not much time left over for writing letters to me back home.

Much of my time was occupied with plans for the Baby Bounce that fall. It was our school's version of a freshmen initiation. It fell short of hazing but allowed us some leeway within our plans for an evening of picking on the new high school arrivals. As a member of the committee planning the event, the attention to detail kept me occupied my first six weeks of that school year. Devising some activity that wound up with all the freshmen in diapers was a staple of the event. By the end of the evening of the Bounce there was no harm, no foul and a good time was had by all.

That Christmas I became much more conscious of how Mike's family celebrated. Their idea of the end of the year event was nothing like what I was used to. I couldn't get over the fact that his brother was given his Christmas present in October. What kind of Christmas Eve would that be for him? They just didn't seem to put as much emphasis on the day as the Newton family. The only positive aspect of my pre-occupation with the Moriarty Christmas was that I never noticed how much time Ma was spending away from the everyday lives of our family. Surely Dad would begin to suspect that Ma's attention was elsewhere.

Dear God, would this ever stop. How would this end? Divorce was never anything we Catholics discussed or considered. But how could this farce go on with so many people aware of their affair.

Father Fitz seemed to be taking over more and more of the parish functions and no one tried to stop that runaway train. He certainly wasn't acting like a man trying to leave the order and settle down with a woman from the parish. Keeping busy and staying out of the house as much as possible became my new mantra.

The television coverage of President Kennedy's inauguration kept most of us glued to our television sets. The Massachusetts native made us feel part of the new Camelot being discussed nonstop. I just wanted to see more of Jacqueline's wardrobe. Knockoffs of her pillbox hats with veils and short white gloves became part of the Sunday morning attire in church. Ma started hiding her new suits with shorter skirts at the back of my closet.

As the January weather turned colder, my classes required more homework. Then the unthinkable happened. Grandpa died. He was working in the boiler room of the church when he suffered a heart attack.

It was the first time I ever saw anyone in a coffin. It hurt to see Granny walking around trying to be strong for the rest of us. They were lucky enough to celebrate their fiftieth wedding anniversary together. Watching their seven children hover around Granny in order to satisfy her every need made me want to have a large family when it was time to think about those things.

Sunday dinners became all the more important. If anything, we lingered longer into the afternoon.

Rehearsals for the Minstrel Show kept me busy for the next six weeks. It would be my first year as a soloist. Dad's usual contribution to the chorus seemed to help with his grieving process, as well. For the next two weeks the entire company joined the rehearsals. That's when the moderator for the show, Father Fitz, became actively involved.

The only saving grace was Ma wasn't a part of the show. But that didn't stop her. She arranged for the Women's Sodality to manage the refreshment stand during the nights of the shows. That meant she would come to the auditorium as the evening rehearsals were ending and get very busy in the kitchen and serving areas preparing the space for their sales. When Dad would ask if she wanted to leave, she always found some task that needed completion. I wondered how she could be so obvious to so many, but not to Dad.

With the success of the show behind us, my concentration was on the end of the year activities, especially my high school graduation.

The Senior Prom was scheduled for the month before

our final exams and graduation. Mike would be home from UMass by that time, and we were all going to one of my classmates' homes for a party after the Prom. Everyone looked forward to the after-Prom activities that would probably keep us partying until the next morning.

We developed the usual senioritis and managed to finish enough academic requirements so as not to embarrass our families.

The morning of the Prom I woke up with my period. I couldn't believe I wouldn't be able to wear my beautiful new gown and matching shawl. Why did I let my friends talk me into such a light-colored gown? By ten o'clock the vomiting began.

Ma even made me some warm milk and crackers to see if it would settle my stomach. In the afternoon she went down to the drug store for a vanilla ice cream cone. In the past I was able to hold one down toward the dry heave part of my curse. Even she knew what a disappointment it would be if I didn't go to my very last dance.

Mike called and we agreed he would still pick up his tuxedo and come for me just before the couples attending the Prom did the walk-around-the-auditorium for the choosing of the King and Queen. It's too bad my gown was white because you couldn't tell where the fabric ended, and my pale skin began. Somehow, with Mike's help, I made it through the night. I never ate a thing even at the after party, but at least I was able to be with my friends during our night of passage.

That summer I found myself feeling faint a lot, especially in church. Our family doctor said it was my nerves and she increased my Librium prescription. I tried to stay active and out of the house as much as possible.

After graduation I was hired full time at the Tuberculosis and Health Association downtown. My responsibilities at the monthly clinics increased and sometimes I would have to drive a newly diagnosed patient to the Tuberculosis Sanatorium out of town.

There was one trip when I was forced to stop the car in front of a bus and run up to the driver to ask for his assistance because the patient I was transporting got out of hand. The patient went from rocking back and forth protesting his diagnosis and eventual hospitalization, to his attempt to turn the car around by sitting on my lap and taking over the wheel. I finally maneuvered the car across two lanes of that backcountry road and stopped a bus as it came toward us from the other direction. The bus driver came over to see if we were hurt and became aware of my problem. With his help I managed to get the patient secure in the passenger seat – no seatbelts back then – so I could drive the rest of the way to the sanatorium without interference. Looking into a different career plan became my new pastime.

I spent most of my time working during the week and going places with Mike on weekends. When I turned eighteen that summer my aunt and uncle taught me how to drive a car and by the time Mike had to go back to school that fall, I had a license and was able to buy a used 1957 Chevy. It was yellow and true to its color, was a real lemon. There was always something wrong with it.

I would drive up through the Notch to Amherst to pick him up on Friday afternoons and drive him back on Sunday nights. We usually stopped for a pizza at the Aqua Fina Restaurant on the top of the mountain. By then, it was the early sixties and young Catholic couples practiced celibacy. So kissing was as far as we went. There was a lot of talk about different boys in our crowd pushing to third base. But, not the good ones, and it was mostly just talk.

It was interesting that Father Fitz had taken that vow but wasn't holding up his end of the bargain.

I started checking to see which priest was saying which Mass on Sunday and avoided the one he celebrated. I also looked for any excuse to be out of the house when I knew he was there. During that entire year I followed that routine. Keeping busy during the weekdays, staying active on weekends, and avoiding Father Fitz at all costs. Even though I did my best to follow that schedule, it didn't mean there was nothing to observe.

A couple of my friends asked me one weekend when we got together whether Ma was still living at home. I didn't understand the question until they admitted that they had seen her with Father Fitz and wondered if Ma and Dad had separated. It obviously would have to change.

I started to think of ways to talk to Dad. It probably was time enough for him to know the truth. I could only imagine what his friends thought about his ignorance and what they must be saying behind his back. Each time I practiced the words I would use to explain the situation to him, I would break out in a sweat. This was not going to be easy.

I managed to avoid the Mass Father Fitz was saying, but no matter which Sunday Mass I attended, feeling faint at some point during the service was becoming a problem.

I thought I would jump out of my skin. I didn't know what was wrong, so I made another appointment with Dr. Daniels.

She couldn't find anything that would account for the problem but said she thought if I stayed in the house with Ma much longer, I would probably be headed for a nervous breakdown. I didn't know anyone who had a nervous breakdown, but it didn't sound like anything I wanted to experience.

That weekend when Mike came home, I told him I thought I might take the civil service exam and apply for a job in Washington, DC. Being alone in a new city was not as bad as being in the one I was trying to avoid.

Before I drove him back to school that weekend, he said "We'll probably get married some day in the future, so why don't we just push up the date and get married next summer after I finish my junior year at the university. I'll finish my last year of study while you work to cover the expenses until I graduate. At least we would be together, and you would be out of the house."

I know –this sounded a lot like the summer we had our first date. We didn't really want this to happen, but why not.

When we told my parents that night Dad said "Fine, if that's what you really want. Father Fitz will marry you."

"Over my dead body," I cried.

Dad was furious and told me he would disown me as a daughter, and I was to gather my things and get out of his house.

There was never any conversation about why I had such feelings about the matter. Maybe he really knew but didn't want to admit it.

For the next few weeks, I stayed at Granny's and went to work from her apartment each day. Ma was still working at The Attic, located only two doors down from Granny's apartment. She never tried to contact me. She knew why I didn't want Father Fitz to marry us. She could have talked to Dad and made things right.

After two weeks I came home one night, and Granny said that she had spoken with Dad, and I should go back home. I was sure that she must have told him about Father Fitz, and he realized why I refused to let him marry me. I was nervous climbing the stairs to the apartment.

To my shock, when I got home that night, Father Fitz was sitting in the parlor with Ma and Dad, and they were all carrying on like nothing had happened. I guess Granny didn't know about the affair either.

It was only a few months after I moved back that Dad bought Ma a house in Longmeadow. It was about twenty minutes away from our Beech Street apartment in Hitchcock, but it might as well have been on Mars.

CHAPTER SEVEN

The new hardwood smell gave the house a cold feeling. There were still boxes to unpack in every room. Dad seemed to think this new house in the country would help to give Ma more comfort in her life. An attempt to quell the shakiness she often displayed.

But I still wasn't convinced this move would really make a difference. She still had to drive my sisters back and forth to their school in Hitchcock each day. They were using Granny's address to make things legal. Driving the girls there was farther than the trips out of town in the past that caused her to call for help because she was too nervous to get home on her own.

When I was able to get ready early enough, I drove them in and then went downtown to my job at the Tuberculosis & Health Association.

Living in Longmeadow was nothing like living on The Knoll in Hitchcock. There were no tenements on the block. There weren't even any blocks. At least not like we were familiar with. Heck they were even void of sidewalks. There were only identical houses ten feet apart with newly planted grass out front. No one walked by at night. The silence was deafening.

It really didn't matter to me. My friends were all working, and we didn't hang out at the park anymore. But my sisters lost out on a lot of their regular after school activities. We didn't know any of the neighbors and it didn't seem like Ma wanted to make new friends.

Within the first two months that we lived there, Ma developed a new pattern that drove me crazy. Each night after supper she said she had to go to one place or another only to return home later and later. I couldn't seem to fall asleep until she returned. Then I would hold my breath while her footsteps echoed as she made her way down the open-backed wooden stairs to the unfinished basement where she hid most her booze. There was still a supply in my bedroom closet, but I guess she didn't want to take the chance that I was still awake. I was petrified that one of those nights she would fall to her death on the new cement basement floor.

Dad was usually sleeping hours before she arrived because he had to leave so early in the morning for work.

I'm not sure how long she sat drinking in the parlor because after she returned to the first floor, I was able to fall asleep.

Father Fitz hadn't been to the new house yet. It was harder to get in the parish car and drive forty minutes out of town at night, than it was to cross the street and sit in the parlor of one of the parishioners. I can't remember seeing him at that Longmeadow house. Maybe something changed. Or maybe he was there during the day when Dad and the rest of us were off completing our daily responsibilities.

On a Friday morning, not long after we settled in, I experienced my monthly female problems. Arriving like clockwork, it continued to cause disturbing physical transformations. The cramps and vomiting never seemed to improve. I kept thinking each new month would be different, but there I was again, a passenger in the police cruiser while another officer followed in my car. I never realized the benefits of having my office so close to the police station when I took that job. My boss just got into a routine of calling the men in blue and handing over my car keys.

When I arrived home, Ma was dressed and waiting at

the door with a suitcase. She seemed more nervous than ever. My early return was not part of her plan for the day. After an immediate trip to the bathroom, I got changed but was afraid to close the door to my room because I didn't know what was happening with Ma. She came down the hall saying, "try a little of this, it will help with the cramps," as she tried to pour some kind of alcohol into a Flintstone jelly glass.

"Ma, please, you know it would just make me vomit more," I pleaded.

My refusal caused her to leave my bedroom quickly. I noticed as I hung up my clothes that she had taken several bottles of liquor from the collection she was hiding in my closet. I wondered if she had them in that suitcase by the kitchen door. I took some medication and tried to sleep in an attempt to skip over the vomiting phase.

The sound of the car door in the driveway jolted me upright. I never heard the house door close. I could see from my window that Ma was in the back seat of a taxi as it left our driveway. I ran to the kitchen to call Dad. Maybe he knew where Ma was going.

"I have no idea what's going on, but I'll be home shortly. Just try to relax and stay calm," he repeated three times. It felt strange waiting for Dad. I didn't feel any more stomach cramps or an urge to vomit. I only remember hearing the song on the radio as she drove away. *"Would you like to swing on a star, carry moonbeams home in a jar."* I couldn't get the song out of my head.

Dad tried to act normal when he arrived, but I could clearly see he was upset. "I think it would be better if I drive you to your aunt's so you will have someone with you while you get through the worst of your problem," he said. He never could say period. But I had no more pain. No nausea. No vomiting. Not even any more bleeding. Everything stopped.

When he picked up my sisters from school, he told them that Ma went to New York with her friend Jo for the weekend. It might have kept them in the dark if Hannah hadn't gone into the city the next day for a birthday party for one of her classmates. "I saw Jo coming out of the drugstore. How could she be with Ma in New York," she cried.

By Wednesday things at home were in chaos. The girls were giving Dad trouble with anything he asked them to do. It was almost a week. Where could Ma be?

Was she in a hospital out of town getting sober?

Wouldn't she have told Dad if that's where she was going? Did she finally decide to leave with Father Fitz? Or could they be off together to start a new life. I didn't want to think of what I was really afraid of. Was she pregnant and going to have an abortion?

I left Saturday morning to busy myself with anything that could keep me away, including a visit to Mike at UMass. Planning for our wedding kept me pre-occupied enough to ease the worry I had about Ma.

When Dr. Daniels warned me about my need to get out of the house before my health was ruined, she couldn't have been more on target. August couldn't come fast enough for me.

As I walked in after work on Monday, I noticed the calm immediately. I wasn't even sure anyone was at home. Taking off my coat, I was sure I heard laughter coming from my parent's bedroom at the end of the hall. When I got to their doorway, I saw Ma, Dad and my two sisters all rolling and laughing on the bed. Dad looked up and spoke softly, "Ma is sorry she left you without saying goodbye last week." Ma never said a word.

I was relieved that she was alive and seemingly well, but her lack of apology made me realize that things hadn't really changed. Two weeks later it all fell into shambles.

I was studying for the civil service exam at the dining room table around ten o'clock that night when the phone rang, and Dad answered. He stood silently listening for some time.

When he got off the phone he said, "I need to borrow your car?"

"Is anything wrong.....?" But before I finished my question, he was out the door.

The girls were both asleep in their rooms, so I knew they were safe. Obviously, it wasn't about one of them. He was back so quickly I didn't have much time to worry. His face was void of color as he told me what happened.

"The police called because the neighbors two streets away complained that a car had been left in front of their house several nights over the last few months," he began. "They wanted the police to have it removed. I drove your car over there to see for myself," he continued.

Before Ma left that night, he asked her to get him some tuna fish for his lunch the next day, while she was out with their car.

"I unlocked the car and took the can of tuna she left on the passenger seat," he said as he sat down on the chair and held his face in his hands. I noticed he had put the tuna can on the counter.

I didn't know what to do. Would she tell him whom she was with? How would he react? Should I call Granny? He started to realize I knew more than I was letting on. I couldn't be the one to tell him after all this time.

I did as he asked and went to my room. But even though he asked me to go to bed, I could only lie on my bed in silence as he waited in the kitchen with the tuna on the counter.

It seemed like hours before I heard Ma pulling the car into the driveway.

CHAPTER EIGHT

I held the pillow over my head when I heard the door open.
I didn't want to hear what was going on in the kitchen. I
only heard muffled sounds. After what seemed like
forever, the sounds got quiet and eventually I fell asleep.

Ma was in bed when I left for work the next morning. I
didn't see Dad for a couple of days because our schedules
overlapped. When we finally saw each other later that
week, I knew he was aware of the affair. He asked me to
go with him to the rectory to ask Pastor O'Malley to have
Father Fitz removed from the parish. I wondered where
priests went when they broke their vow of chastity.

Pastor O'Malley listened to Dad's request without
saying a word. He probably was expecting this visit for a
long time. With so many in the parish aware of the affair,
it wouldn't be surprising for someone to have said something to him by now. He was very quiet when he finally
spoke. "We'll need to contact Bishop Weldon on this
matter," he declared. "For the time being I will put him on
administrative leave. He will not be saying Mass this

weekend." He just took our word for the accusation. Didn't he want to run this by Father Fitz? Or did he know better? I looked at Dad's face as he spoke to Pastor O'Malley. There were tears welling up in his eyes, but he willed himself to hold them back as he stood and shook hands on our way out of the rectory. I wanted to grab Dad and give him a hug as we walked back to our car, but hugging was foreign to our family. Not something I ever remember experiencing. Instead, I just offered to drive, and he accepted.

It was several weeks before Father Fitz left the parish. The word was that he was sent somewhere in the Boston area. The diocese of Springfield, Massachusetts included parishes from the western part of the state, which meant that Bishop Weldon had to approve the transfer. I don't think it mattered that he had been the Bishop whose ring I kissed when I received my confirmation just a few years earlier. I'm sure this wasn't his only personnel issue he had to fix.

Soon after Father Fitz's transfer, it felt like there was a truce of sorts around our house. Dad and Ma seemed to be going through a period of reconciliation. But life in the house in Longmeadow came to an end. We moved. Maybe it was part of the new agreement between Ma and Dad, or maybe it was just an attempt at a fresh start.

After we moved back on The Knoll in Hitchcock - this time to an apartment building on Walnut Street - I spent most of my time working on wedding plans. We chose our attendants and selected gowns and flowers. The menu was tasted, and the wedding cake ordered.

Ma and I spoke for the first time in years with responses other than yes and no. She hosted a bridal shower for me and worked with Mike's mother on one she had planned. Back then it was common to have several showers to make sure the bride and groom received enough gifts to begin housekeeping. There was even something we called a 'joint party." It's not the same kind of joint we refer to today. It meant that both the bride and groom were honored before their wedding and the monies collected at the door for the dance and buffet would be given to the couple to start their married life.

Ma had put on some weight over the last year and I looked at that as a good sign. It was probably the most family-like lifestyle I can remember from my double-digit years and beyond. Ma and Dad even seemed to be talking more often and they actually went out on the weekend a few times before I took my wedding vows and left for my new life.

The wedding took place on the last weekend of August. The high temperature at ten in the morning made the air feel muggy. The temperature wasn't much cooler inside as Dad escorted me down the long aisle to meet my husband-to-be. There were several fans blowing on their highest settings placed throughout the upstairs church.

I knelt with my groom and our attendants on the special kneelers placed on the altar for such occasions. The fan blew my veil to the right and covered the back of Mike's white jacket. I began to feel faint. A bride with her head between her legs was not a pretty sight. Somehow, we were able to complete the ceremony and become official in the eyes of the Church.

When we got outside on our way to the limo that would take us to our reception, my new husband asked me to promise to turn over my bottle of Librium.

I was a little surprised by the request.

"I'm not sure you'll like the me without them," I said.

"Let's gamble on the fact that we will both like the you without them," Mike said with an edge of confidence.

I haven't had one since that morning in 1963.

The reception was held at the Chateau Harmony in Granby and was attended by over one hundred guests. Dad looked handsome as we danced our dance and Ma was in her glory. She appeared happier than I could ever remember.

Late in the afternoon I changed into my Jacqueline Kennedy Pill Box hat and matching cranberry going-away-suit. Of course, I had the proper white gloves to accessorize the outfit. Ma had a little influence in the choice. It felt good to shop together.

There were lots of well wishes as we left the reception, but no kiss good-bye from either Dad or Ma. Kissing good-bye and saying 'I love you" wasn't part of our modus operand. It hadn't happened up to that point in my family and would have been surprising if it happened on my wedding day.

We drove to Hamden, Connecticut that night on our way to the Pocono Mountains.

About an hour after we checked into our room, my new husband asked if I thought I might want to remove my gloves and hat while I was sitting on the bed watching television. It was the sixties. I was a Catholic. We didn't have pre-marital sex. It was a strange and somewhat uncomfortable night. There were no books or classes about wedding night sex and there had been no "talk" from Ma about married birds or bees.

By the time we returned from our honeymoon in the Pocono Mountains we had consummated our marriage and we began practicing rhythm when we returned to Hitchcock. It would be our first night in our new apartment on Oak Street in the valley.

I wanted to make a special dinner for Mike for our first meal in our new kitchen. Ma never had any recipes that I knew of, and Granny wasn't home, so I found a recipe in a magazine for meatloaf.

It took quite some time to complete but it tasted great. The only problem was that we had meatloaf for the rest of the month. I didn't realize the recipe was figured for a gathering of twelve.

Mike commuted to UMass each weekday and I carpooled to the Springfield Armory. I had taken the civil service exam after all and became a GS2. The Armory was the primary center for the manufacture of firearms in the United States, chosen by George Washington and Henry Knox. Today it is western Massachusetts' only National Park and features the world's largest collection of historic firearms.

Dad had been working in the factory for several years at that time and thought it would be a perfect place for his daughter to start a new career.

Getting hired as a secretary to Colonel Bernhard Gehring was a real coo and I wanted to make sure he wasn't sorry, taking special care with everything I was asked to complete.

My life was busy and relaxed, and I even talked to Ma a few times on the phone. I was beginning to think things were going to rise to a level we hadn't seen before.

One Friday morning a few months later I took the call for Colonel Gehring that put the entire complex in a spin. President Kennedy had been shot and every military installation in the country responded. By the end of the day, we were told that he had died. The flag over the entrance of our building was lowered to half-mast, and everyone was crying in the parking lot.

For the next few days, we were all glued to our television sets. All eyes were on Jacqueline Kennedy as she stood with her two young children at their father's wake. Her young son saluted as his father's coffin passed.

Vice-President Johnson had been sworn in as our new

President as the country tried to heal.

The holidays that year were one of the most remembered from my past, my first holiday as a married woman. My determination to change the way Mike celebrated the holiday began in earnest that year. I think the transformation took.

When we divorced twenty-three years later, his family continued to share a huge celebration on Christmas Eve. Because our children were accustomed to the Moriarty event. I was the one who had to reinvent a new tradition on Christmas Eve.

In February we got the call that Dad was in the Hitchcock Hospital. When we got there that night he was waiting for the results of the biopsy from a lump on his neck. The next couple of days we worried as we waited for the diagnosis to come back.

It was Hodgkin's disease. I never heard of it before. The doctors explained it's a form of cancer of the lymph nodes. They felt it was still in the early stages, but there wasn't a cure. He could have years or maybe only weeks.

For the next six weeks, our daily schedule included a visit to the hospital each night after work. Mike thought I was getting fat. I had gained 16 pounds since our wedding. It might have been my own cooking. "Maybe if you run up the stairs to your dad's room each night it might help take off some of that extra weight," Mike chuckled.

Eventually Dad went home with a diagnosis of terminal, but not fatally eminent cancer, and we all tried to return to our former routine.

That month during Dad's hospital stay my period caused me more problems than usual. I thought that after I got married it would not be as bad each month. The doctor said it would be better after I had a baby. The cramps had me doubled over long enough that I had to call my new gynecologist. He said my complaints sounded symptomatic of a miscarriage, but with my previous history, it was most likely just another month with a little more pain. The nurses couldn't fit me into the schedule for several weeks.

By the time I got into his office for an examination, he confirmed that I had in fact had a miscarriage. But he still couldn't give me a D&C because he thought I was pregnant again - so much for the practice of rhythm. His suggestion was to repeat the examination in a month in order to confirm the pregnancy.

Two weeks later Mike came home with the need for a

change in plans.

He got offered a job in Washington, DC after graduation and we left the day after the ceremony.

I was reluctant to leave when Dad was terminal, but I had an obligation to my husband now. And besides, Ma was on her best behavior. I didn't realize it wouldn't last long. A few days before we left for our new life, the movers arrived and packed up our belongings for the move. That night we found ourselves opening several of the boxes because they packed Mike's cap and gown. You had to watch them every minute.

CHAPTER NINE

Vomiting in the Baltimore-Washington tunnel was not the way to spend the eighth hour of our trip. We traveled through the night and speeding by those cement blocks made my eyes flicker until the feeling arrived in my stomach.

The gynecologist must be right. I was pregnant. I was sure it was morning sickness and I needed to find a gynecologist first thing.

Could we really be moving to the nation's capital? I had never been this far south before. Mike would be working on Pennsylvania Avenue just down the street from President Johnson. If our friends could see us now, I thought.

We only had a few days after we arrived before Mike needed to begin his new career. We found a two-bedroom garden apartment at Buckingham Estates in Arlington, VA, near the corner of Pershing Drive and Glebe Road.

Most of the residents were transplants from the north

except the older couple living next door. He was from West Virginia, and she was from Georgia. It was the first time I experienced real bigotry. I never heard that kind of insults towards blacks before. They were otherwise very nice and neighborly. She came and placed onions cut in half on all my windowsills the week they painted the hallways. She said, "It could harm the baby you're carrying." I wondered if this was a southern old wives tale. She really meant well.

The young couple downstairs was friendly enough. They would smile and say hello when we came into the building. I wished I had a job to go to, but Mike wouldn't hear of his wife having to work while pregnant. Until the baby I was carrying was old enough to leave with a babysitter, I would have to settle for being pregnant and accepting of my new life in Virginia.

The day I turned twenty-one I was four months pregnant. Mike had to take the train to a company meeting in Pennsylvania and wouldn't be back until at least midnight. I was feeling sorry for myself when Dad called with well wishes.

"Your mother is out of town for the week," he said softly. "I know she wants you to enjoy your birthday."

I didn't like the sound of that assumption. "Where did she go," I asked holding my breath.

"I think she's in Atlantic City with some of her girlfriends," he replied.

He didn't know, I thought. Could the affair be starting up again? "When will she be back," I asked?

"Not sure, but certainly by the weekend" he said with determination.

I wasn't convinced.

I went to the bakery and ordered a birthday cake, had them write Happy Birthday Trisha on the top and I took it home.

The next day I was outed when my neighbor downstairs asked whom I was singing to the night before. After singing to myself, I cut a piece for Mike, left it on a plate, and ate the rest. I blamed it on the pregnancy. I really missed home.

My regular routine was to go to my weekly obstetric appointment, weigh in, and stop at the bakery in the same strip mall on my way home for a delicious dessert. There wasn't much else to do in the new town and I missed my friends at the Armory back home. Mike was so busy trying to get established in his new career he didn't have a lot of time to spend keeping me company. His regular trips out of town were not always supportive of a pregnant woman.

The fact that I would get into our recliner to watch television and was trapped in there until he got home to help me out, wasn't helpful. The weight from the baby settled in the chair and held me in place. There were also times when I got down on the floor to select a can of vegetables out of the lower cabinets and had to remain there until Mike got home from work. I gained forty pounds during that pregnancy – more than a third of my total weight.

We eventually became friendly with a couple from New England who lived across the quad. They had two children and she was someone I could talk to about my pregnancy. She never asked why I wasn't informed of some of the most basic mother-in-waiting concerns, but she knew I never talked about my mother.

Ma had never called, and she was never around when I phoned home. She started staying away from their apartment more. I was worried about how Dad could handle his illness and my two sisters without any help. But, by then I was in my third trimester and not allowed to travel home for a visit. The hardest part was not being able to go home for Christmas. I remember wearing a red maternity coatdress. The temperature was eighty degrees and Mike and I had Christmas dinner at a wonderful restaurant in Washington, DC. But there was no snow, no caroling and no family gathering.

That morning our next-door neighbors invited us to come across the hall for a Christmas drink. He poured bourbon straight into small glasses and handed them around. Thank goodness I could use my pregnancy as an excuse to refuse the offer. She showed me all her gifts she got that day. I wondered why she wrapped up all the gifts she bought after we shopped together at the mall and opened them that day. I guess that was her tradition. Not one I wanted to emulate.

Our new friends across the quad were both professionals. She was an attorney and had to fly north to give a deposition one week while her husband was also traveling. They asked if I would watch their six-year-old son for the day. He developed a nickname in the neighborhood as the local Dennis the Menace, but I wanted to be a generous neighbor, so I agreed to the job.

My trouble began in the afternoon when he threw his favorite toy in the mailbox on the corner and when went in after it. He couldn't get out by himself. At seven months pregnant, there was no way I could lift him out either. It was only with the help of the local fire department that he was rescued. Needless to say, there weren't any more requests from his parents for babysitting.

Dad called regularly and we talked for hours. His relationship with Ma was not good. She would go off for days at a time. He told me that she was in Atlantic City again with her friends. I didn't believe him. I held out a secret hope that she might come a little further on the train to visit us in Virginia. She never came. She never called. We never talked.

On February 1st, after thirteen hours of labor, I delivered an eight-pound twelve-ounce baby girl. They called her the den mother of the nursery. We called her Maura.

The hospital had only one bathroom on the maternity floor. Every woman had to stand in a long line to make use of it. The first time I stood in the line I passed out. After that, the doctor left orders that I was not to go to the bathroom without the assistance of a nurse.

That afternoon, I pushed my call button for nearly a half hour without anyone responding. All I could do was call Dad. "I'm in such pain. I'm afraid I am going to wet this bed," I cried. "Is Ma around? Can she come to the phone?" I was hoping Ma had some helpful suggestions for getting through the required one-week-stay in that hospital. "She's not here now. I'll have her call you if she returns soon," was the only thing he could say. I knew she wouldn't call.

Four weeks later, Dad and Granny flew down to Washington, DC for my daughter's baptism, along with my aunt and uncle who would be her Godparents. If they were kind enough to teach me how to drive, they could probably oversee my daughter's spiritual life should the need ever arise. And besides, there was no one else we knew well enough to ask from Virginia. We were too new in town.

Dad said Ma wasn't at home much at the time. She was a grandmother for the first time. I didn't understand why she wouldn't want to see her granddaughter. She didn't come to the baptism. We christened our daughter Maura Moriarty. Mike didn't want to give her a middle name. He felt she should choose one of her liking when she was confirmed as a teenager. She was such a good baby. She probably knew her mother didn't have much experience.

Three months later Mike was offered a job at a Massachusetts computer company and we jumped at the chance to get back to New England. While it wasn't Hitchcock, it was only an hour and a half down the Massachusetts turnpike.

We found an apartment and moved into a two-building complex in the Italian neighborhood of Framingham. Within two weeks of our arrival, we found friends in the building next door. Jan had a son close to my daughter's age and we would take them for daily walks in their carriages.

But there was something not quite right about Jan. She seemed to be daydreaming a lot. She would come to my apartment daily and try to give her son a bottle of milk that had been in his carriage for hours. The milk would curdle right in the bottle. Several times I called her house and heard her son crying, nearly screaming, and she never seemed to hear him.

I finally found the courage to talk to her husband about my concerns. He took her to the Framingham Union Hospital for a medical diagnosis.

One afternoon a few weeks later he asked if I could watch their son while they went for some procedure. When they got back Jan didn't know me. Her mother came from out of town, and I never saw much of her after that. Her husband told us she was getting shock therapy for something called the "baby blues."

We would visit our families in Hitchcock as often as we could get away. Dad wasn't doing well. The Hodgkin's was advancing. He wasn't able to work anymore and had to go on disability.

I found out I was pregnant with my second child, and we started looking for a house. She was the result of a desired pregnancy - the only one we planned. That pregnancy, for the most part, was without incident but going back and forth to Hitchcock did take its toll.

The phone rang one afternoon, and I heard my sister Hannah's voice saying, "Dad's dead." Then she hung up. We still had only one car and it was in the parking lot at work with Mike. By the time he got home and picked me up and we drove to Hitchcock, Dad had started to feel better. There were no cell phones then, so we only found out after we arrived at his apartment. Ma had moved out by then and Dad never said where she went. I'm not sure he knew.

We wondered if he was going to get a divorce, but

Catholics didn't even speak the word in the sixties, never mind do the deed. My greater concern was how my sisters would be able to deal with Dad's illness as it progressed.

Our two-bedroom apartment was getting crowded, and we wanted more room for our expanding family. A yard with a swing set was something our two-year-old would appreciate when that new baby prevented us from going on our daily trip to the park. We bought a three-bedroom ranch with a full basement in an older neighborhood of Framingham.

Two months later my second daughter arrived on a hot Sunday in June. She was three weeks late and the nurses in the labor room had me convinced there was a problem. For the first hour after I arrived in the hot labor room with no air conditioning, I watched the nurses look at each other with concern as they continued to monitor my contractions. After they paged my doctor out of the delivery room, I asked them what was happening. "We think we hear three heartbeats," the taller one stated as fact. The room got hotter.

The doctor rushed in, mask still covering his face, and took a listen for himself. "She just has big babies," he told them. In my second month of pregnancy, I was measured to see how big a baby I would be able to deliver. Twenty-six pounds was their finding. All I could think of was that I was going to have a twenty-six-pound baby.

Erin weighed in at eight pounds, eleven and a half ounces, just a half an ounce smaller than her two-year-old sister weighed at birth.

There is some truth to the saying "you're not a family until you have two children". I think it has something to do with when one is sleeping the other is awake and vice versa. Anyway, I was adjusting to having a second towhead around the house. Ma had still not seen Erin. There was no call or card after she was born. My sister Connie and Mike's brother Joe agreed to become her godparents and even on that special day only Dad came to the observe her receipt of that sacrament.

For the first time since I became a married woman, I really got involved with my surroundings. Joining the Newcomers Club was my first attempt at the suburban lifestyle.

It's funny how things just snowball and before you know it, you're running things. It started with an agreement to serve on the membership committee. The chairman moved out of town and after only three months

I was in charge of attracting new residents to our monthly gatherings.

I found out from a former classmate that Ma was living in the valley of Hitchcock on Acorn Street. After several attempts at contacting her, she agreed to let us come by with our two daughters on a Sunday afternoon. It would be the first time she would see our newest daughter.

The third-floor walk-up had a funny odor as we climbed the stairs. Nothing like the smell of Granny's roast beef. When she opened the door, I didn't think I could move at first. She had changed since the last time I saw her. Thirty pounds thinner would be a generous estimate. There were dark circles under her eyes and her pupils had a red cast. Her clothing hadn't caught up to her weight loss. The apartment was sparse and there were several bottles of liquor on the kitchen counter. There didn't appear to be anyone else living in the apartment with her.

After a few comments about the weather, I asked her why she was living like that. Why she left Dad. Why did she think that my two teenage sisters were capable of taking care of Dad by themselves? How come she never wanted to see my daughters?

Her only response was, "I hope you're never as sick as

I am."

"What does that mean," I asked. "What do you have?"

When it became clear that she would not be clearing up any of my confusion about her choices, I told her that Dad was not doing well and could use her companionship or at least a visit.

Her, "I'll see what I can do. I think I'll be moving soon," response was not comforting.

I knew then that he was not going to see her again before he died. What I didn't know was that I would never see her again before she died. I never told Dad about my visit. It was better for him to think she might return at any time. They had been doing that dance for a number of years. Her pattern was well developed. Why force him to give up the hope of one more go-round.

That Christmas Dad joined us in Framingham to be with his granddaughters for one last visit from Santa. We all knew he was going downhill faster than we wanted to admit. Connie got engaged that Christmas and announced that she would be getting married in August. Dad told her when it came time to send out invitations to the wedding, Ma's name could be printed with his, but she was not allowed to attend the wedding. I think he was hoping that would jolt her into returning home.

That was the first time I felt any emotion coming from him as a result of her new life choices. I did feel sorry for Connie though. It is awful going through a major life experience without your mother.

The first weekend in June, a few days before Erin turned one year old, we decided to drive to Hitchcock and have a little celebration with Dad and my sisters. Hannah would be graduating from high school later that week and it was the only time I could see her before her big day.

One of our favorite take-out meals as a family on The Knoll was the spaghetti and meatballs from Mel's with a side order of their phenomenal crinkle cut French fries. Dad wanted to do something special for Erin and Hannah, so he placed the order and took Maura with him to pick up our Sunday dinner.

He'd been gone longer than ever when he finally arrived with a scrape on his left arm. "Dad, what happened to you" we spoke in unison.

"Grandpa fell out of the car," Maura offered.

There were no seatbelts in cars back then, and children were allowed to sit anywhere in the car. But at least Maura was in the back seat when the other car ran into Dad's and spun them around in the middle of the intersection, causing the driver's door to pop open. Dad's body was forced out and he landed on his left arm, but his right foot remained curled around the brakes. He could only think of Maura in the back seat and refused to let his body leave the car.

I'm sure his injuries from that accident accelerated any cancer lying dormant inside of him. We wanted him to get checked out at the hospital, but he felt he would be fine and thought he'd spent enough time in the Hitchcock Hospital for a while.

Later that week I called him on the pretense of discussing Bobby Kennedy's assassination, when I really wanted to find out about his health. We both agreed it was hard to believe that another of our beloved Massachusetts' Kennedy's was killed. Poor Rose - another son to bury.

Dad's health report was not convincing. I was sure he had upset the applecart enough to require a visit at least to his doctor. But he was stubborn and refused to have things checked out. Deep down he knew it was bad.

Two weeks later he danced at my cousin's wedding, but that turned out to be his last public social event. He was admitted to the hospital a week later. For the next two months he remained hospitalized. He never came home again.

We traveled down the Mass Pike to see him every weekend over that summer. The doctors would only give medical updates to me. Ma would have been the one to hear from his doctors, but they were up to speed on her whereabouts and knew any attempt to reach her was useless. It was so hard watching him whittle away that forty-pound loss since the accident.

He had several friends visiting him over that summer. They would be joking with him whenever I walked into his hospital room. There were several days when Dad would have fluid pumped from his lungs. We never knew what we would find upon arrival.

"Hi Buster, are you here to see Dad," I asked Dad's friend, as I walked off the elevator. He looked at me like I was crazy. Why else would he be standing with one foot in Dad's room?

"They told me I could wait here while they got him back in his bed," he said. "I spoke with him on the phone last night. He said he would love to see me and catch up on old times. I had no idea he was this sick" he whispered under his breath.

Dad must not have had a good night. He sounded good

to us as well, when we called yesterday. But things changed quickly with him. A few minutes later, the attendants left the room with their equipment and Dad called us inside. The doctor told me they sometimes experience a surge just before the end. It appeared as though the surge had dissipated. His color was as gray as the cardboard in the shirts from the cleaners.

Buster could see that Dad was having a hard time breathing so he told him he could only stay for a minute. "I'm on my way to a doctor's appointment," he said unconvincingly.

Dad always said the same thing when one of his friends would leave his room, "see you down the Jess." It was the local hangout the men from The Knoll would frequent.

"See you there soon," Buster said smiling as he left the room. None of Dad's friends were fooled. They just let him pretend things were going to be fine.

Dad never talked about his prognosis and wouldn't allow us to have conversations of that nature or to even put a period on the end of a negative thought. His strength was amazing.

Then there was that matter of his daughter's wedding

in a few short weeks. He made it clear that even though he would probably not be home for the occasion and would most likely be forced to have his brother walk my sister, Connie, down the aisle, there was no reason why she couldn't be given the same kind of family involvement in her wedding events as I had for mine. That's when he asked me to stand-in for Ma.

What he really wanted was a hostess at his apartment for coffee and pastries after the wedding at the church and for light refreshments after the reception ended in the ballroom. Normally the parents of the bride would invite family and friends to their house after the bridal couple left on their honeymoon.

This would mean making sandwiches and salads for about forty people in a kitchen I hadn't used for years. But there was no way I could refuse this request from Dad.

CHAPTER TEN

"We're taking him off of all life support today." The words I had feared for the last twelve weeks.

"But, doctor, tomorrow is my sister's wedding" I pleaded. "Couldn't we keep him on a few more days?"

Connie's wedding plans had caused many a sleepless night since Dad was admitted to the hospital. The progression of Hodgkin's didn't allow him any relief from the constant fluid drains and platelet replacements. Each time I thought he might be released a new tumor would appear on his neck or chest.

This week was exceptionally draining because of all the preparation Dad wanted me to oversee. I could have used Ma's help, but Dad's refusal to let her attend the wedding put the cabash on that. I couldn't believe she wouldn't be there for her daughter's wedding. She left for good between Dad's first diagnosis four years earlier and Connie's engagement. I wondered if she ever contacted Connie after her engagement announcement was in the paper. Connie never talked about it.

I was not only filling her "mother-of-the-bride" duties, but my three-year-old daughter, Maura, was the flower girl and had been sporting a hundred and three fever for the last forty-eight hours. Now this.

I didn't know what to tell Connie when she returned from her rehearsal? Maybe nothing. A bride should not walk down the aisle worrying that her father might be dead before she said, 'I do.' She needed to be able to leave on her honeymoon without worrying about having to return on a moment's notice.

"I heard you talking to the Doctor," my sister Hannah whispered over my shoulder as I hung up the phone. She had just returned from the rehearsal and started helping with the food preparation for the next day.

Several of our extended family would come to Dad's apartment after the reception. A buffet for them and out of town guests was the expected normal in our neck of the woods. For as long as I could remember it was usually made and served by the parents of the bride. That's where I came into the picture and, anything I could prepare ahead of time was a bonus.

"I was just asking the doctor what time the limo could pick Dad up tomorrow" I lied. Hannah would be living in this apartment by herself and I worried about what that meant. Anytime she called for help, my drive back home with two toddlers in the car was always a challenge. But my new concern was making sure she was able to handle what life was throwing her way. Ma had left us in charge of Dad's healthcare. Come to think of it, she left us in charge of just about everything. What the hell was she thinking?

"I know the Doctor only talks to you about important medical decisions, but now that I'm out of high school I can handle that responsibility," Hannah assured me. No one could convince me that an eighteen-year-old, two months beyond high school graduation, should carry such decisions on her shoulders. "Well, let's just get through tomorrow and we can decide what happens next" I replied. "But, at least for now, let's keep the Doctor's call to ourselves. Connie doesn't need to know anything tonight."

Mike was holding our three-year-old daughter on his left hip when he joined us in the kitchen. He had gone with her to the wedding rehearsal.

"She walked up the aisle, holding on to the ring bearer with one arm and the flower bouquet with the other. If they ask her to throw petals, all bets are off," he laughed. "The look on her face was one of panic, but no one would ever guess she was still battling a fever."

"As long as she gets down the aisle without incident, it will be good enough for me," I informed Mike. Whose bright idea was it to put a three-year-old in a pale-yellow dress? Obviously, someone without kids.

The ceremony went off without a hitch. Maura performed her duties holding the arm of my five-year old cousin. They looked like miniature prom-goers. After they got down the aisle, she sat with her back to the ceremony so she could see if I was behind her in the church. And, as Mike warned the night before, she walked out of church with a look of fright on her face that brought chuckles from the family and friends watching the wedding party leave the church behind the new bride and groom.

The warm August morning allowed for lingering outside the church as the wedding guests shot multiple variations of pictures. Each of them convinced Dad would want every remembrance they could record.

I left Mike in charge of the flower girl while I ran back to get the coffee and donuts in Dad's apartment ready for the extended family. The phone was ringing as I unlocked the door. "Trisha, I'm not feeling well enough to have the bridal party come to the hospital for those pictures Connie wants." He was getting worse. "I'll tell her you're having some unexpected tests Dad. Can I still send the limo to get you for the reception?" I held my breath. His voice was so weak. "I'll be ready when it arrives," he said with what sounded like a frog in his throat.

I heard footsteps climbing the stairs in the hallway. The guests had arrived. The food needed to be displayed. The ice needed to be placed in buckets for those wanting more than coffee. This role as mother-of-the-bride was getting the best of me. I hated her for placing us all in this situation. If she hadn't cheated on him, if she hadn't left him again and again, he wouldn't have banned her from this event.

"Hello. You look warm. Can I get you something to drink," I repeated several times over the next two hours until it was finally time to leave for the next phase of the celebration - the reception.

When the limo arrived at the front door of the ballroom, Dad was rolled into the room in a wheelchair. It was made for a child. All seventy pounds of him fit onto one half of the seat. He didn't want the child strap that came with the chair, but everyone could see it hanging and buckled around the back. There were a lot of wet faces in the ballroom, especially when it became obvious that there would be no segment of bride-dancing-with-her-father to the traditional rendition of *Daddy's Little Girl*.

I found Hannah in the bathroom sobbing. "He's dying," was all I could understand between her sobs. She knew things were sliding downhill. Nothing I could say made her feel better. I knew what came next. When the reception was over, they would take Dad back to the hospital, Connie would leave on her honeymoon and by the next morning, I would be heading back to Framingham with my husband and daughters. I wanted Hannah to come home with me. The next few days would be tough for her, and I wouldn't be back until the following weekend, unless I got a call from the hospital. But the one thing that made my stomach turn was that Hannah should not be alone for the next seventy-two hours. She had her mind made up. She was determined to stay and visit Dad daily. I hated Ma.

The next week flew by. I tried catching up with all that happened back in Framingham. Things I put off, while preparing for the wedding. Then I spent hours rescheduling all the required meetings at daycare for the fall schedule.

There was also the trip to the mall to buy black attire for what I knew would be just a matter of time. But no matter how many attempts I made I could not bring myself to buy the black dress. Maybe I thought if I didn't have one, I wouldn't need one.

When we pulled into the driveway at my mother-in-law's the following weekend, my breathing pattern had almost returned to normal. But it was not long for this world.

Mike's mother was standing outside, waving her hands over her head, when we pulled up to the back door. Before we could even get out of the car, she was yelling, "Get right to the hospital. They just called looking for you. They are giving your father the last rites."

"Oh my God. Not yet. I'm not ready to let him go", I kept repeating.

She took the girls into the house and told us she had them covered for as long as we needed.

Mike and I drove through two red lights before we arrived in the hospital parking lot.

When we got off the elevator on Dad's floor, I could see activity outside his door. Dad's brothers and sisters were there. They moved out of my way as I got to the room and my shock was seeing Dad sitting up in his bed.

I always thought that when someone was given the last rites one would either be in a coma or at least lying down in pretty bad shape.

Dad was asking Hannah "Do you see that sign up there?" pointing to the television hanging on the wall.

Hannah turned from her spot on the end of Dad's bed and after a few seconds, she responded with "Yeah."

"Well," he sat up straight, "it says this is Hannah's bed."

She nervously started biting her fingernails and Mike asked her if she would like to go down to the cafeteria for a coke. When they left the room, I took over Hannah's spot on the bed.

"You gave us a scare," I told Dad. "They said the priest was called to give you a fine send off."

"Only the good die young" he said.

I couldn't imagine anyone else thinking that forty-nine was old, or was he thinking he was bad?

"But listen," he said, "before Mike and Hannah get back, I want to ask you something."

"What is it, Dad?"

He pushed himself up to nearly a sitting position. "I

need to know that if anything does happen, you'll take care of Hannah." He spoke like a man on a mission. I'll never forget that look in his eyes.

"Without question" I replied. "Now let's see if we can make you more comfortable. You look like you're preparing for a tumbling competition." He wasn't fooling anyone. He was even too weak to roll over on his own.

Mike and Hannah came back in the room just in time to help me lift Dad long enough to straighten out his sheets and lower him down without that bunching he was laying on before.

"I just left a message with the airlines for Connie and her new husband, Randy to come directly to the hospital after they landed," Hannah reported.

We told our new brother-in-law, before they left the reception last week, that there might be a message at their hotel on the islands during the week. Thankfully, we didn't have to make that call. We could see that Dad was starting to fade in and out and we worried that Connie might not get to see him before it was too late.

Just as it was getting dark, Connie and Randy walked into the room. Dad had made it until she returned. He listened to all the news from their island honeymoon and then fell asleep peacefully. But he continued to fight silently.

The next morning Dad was in what the doctors called a static state. I thought it was really a coma. At least he never came out of whatever state he was in. Never spoke to us again. We were warned that the hearing is the last sense to go, and we should not say things in his room we wouldn't want him to hear. We waited by his bedside for the next two days.

Mike finally had to return to work on Tuesday because the doctors said Dad could go on like this for days. We only brought enough clothing for the one-day visit on Sunday and we had already stretched their capabilities. The girls were running out of everything. We decided to go back to Framingham. Mike returned to work, and my best friend took me shopping for the black dress for Dad's funeral. There was no more denial on my part.

When I returned to Hitchcock the next day with the girls, we spent most of our time at my aunts. She was able to watch the girls for me so I could spend my time in the hospital with Dad. Hannah was staying with another aunt during Dad's final days. In fact, she had been there since the wedding last week.

She shared my concern for Hannah's future and wanted to help. On Friday morning, the call from the nurses' station at 7:00 a.m. woke everyone up.

"We don't think you should come to the hospital this morning. Your father is not in a state that you should see right now, especially by yourself."

I wondered if they would have said that to Ma if she were the responsible party of record. At twenty-five, I was a lot stronger than they thought. But I didn't have the energy to argue. And besides, my girls were now wide awake, and my aunt would gladly accept the extra pair of hands to get them dressed and fed.

By 10:30 when the phone rang my aunt didn't even try to answer the call. We both knew what it was about. Sure enough, Dad had died. They said his body would be ready to be released in a couple of hours.

"Which funeral director do you want us to call," I heard the nurse ask on the other end of the line. I didn't have an answer.

My uncles came and helped me get through the rest of the day. There was the obituary that needed to be written for the newspaper. When it came time to list the people Dad left behind, no one felt we should list Ma. He surely didn't leave her. We didn't even know where or if she was living. She hadn't made any calls to the hospital. No visits. No cards. Dad never once spoke her name during his twelve-week stay.

After the obituary was called into the paper, the necessary flowers were ordered, and we left for the funeral home. It was the first time I ever saw coffins lined up for the choosing. I guess I always thought they just miraculously appeared in time to tuck the body tightly inside.

The decisions about limos needed for family, prayers to be read during the funeral mass, and what music would be played throughout the ceremony were decided with very little hesitation. My body felt like it was made of granite. I had trouble moving from one place to another. Why couldn't she at least show up for his funeral? They promised to love and cherish each other until death. I think they should change the vows to include at least one week after death. My only thought was that maybe Ma had already died. There could be no other explanation.

Mike returned from Framingham and picked up the girls from my aunts and brought them to his mother's. She would be taking care of them for the next three days.

That night I spent just holding them and getting lost in their tales of woe. It was such a reprieve from the day's activities. It allowed me to think of something, anything, other than where my parents were that night.

The family was allowed into the funeral home to view the body before the doors were opened to any of the people waiting in line outside. He looked twenty years younger than he did the last time I saw him. That embalming fluid worked miracles. It even added forty pounds to the frail skeleton that was wheeled into Connie's wedding reception just two weeks earlier.

The calling hours were from two to four and seven to nine for the next two days. Because he was one of seven children and because they had all remained in the same geographical area their whole lives, the flowers filled three rooms and the lines of callers never stopped. By four o'clock we were able to see the end of the line and we left for supper within the hour.

The August air outside was warm but refreshing. I was almost ready to man the battle station two hours later until we looked at the guest book that was set up at the entrance of the funeral home. There was a place for guests to sign to inform the funeral attendants about how many people were planning to attend the funeral. It gave the funeral director an idea of how many cars they would need to line up for the ride to the church and how early the procession would need to leave in order to be on time for the funeral Mass. The last line of the ledger was filled in by Ma. She didn't check the box for funeral, but it was definitely her signature.

When we went into the room where Dad was laid out, we saw she had placed her wedding ring in the coffin. My sisters and I went looking throughout all the other rooms in the funeral home. Maybe she went into another room to wait for us to get back. Nope. No Ma. She was gone. Again.

Several times over the next day and a half we would overhear someone mention that they noticed Ma's entry in the guest book. It's a regular process for people looking to see if they can carpool to the church and burial ground. But, by then most people who knew the family would never bring up her name in our presence.

The morning of the funeral, Mike and I walked on either side of Hannah, leading the procession down the long aisle to the front of the church.

Connie and Randy followed next and then all Dad's

brothers and sisters and their families. They supported Granny as they surrounded her. It must be horrible to follow your child in a coffin.

"You don't think Father Fitz would have the nerve to be on the altar this morning?" Hannah asked as we walked toward the family pew.

"If he is Dad will sit up in the coffin" I replied.

The church was nearly full of neighbors and friends of the Newtons. The tears shed that morning were for the relief from the pain that Dad would no longer have to endure. His coffin was placed in the Newton family plot next to his father. There were names on the gravestone with the birth dates and the dates of their deaths left blank for those members who were still living. There was no name or space left for Ma.

During the long ride back from the cemetery in Morrisville I told Hannah I could use her help back in Framingham for a couple of weeks and maybe we could talk about her future plans. She wasn't buying my reasoning. She knew I was trying to get her out of town. But she finally agreed to come back with us that night. After two weeks of catching up with my friends and neighbors and organizations that I was involved with, things finally seemed to calm down.

The nightly discussions we had with Hannah usually ended with more questions than answers. Mike offered to turn the basement of our three-bedroom ranch into a separate apartment for her. She would even have her own entrance. He even went so far as to agree to support her through a court stenographer certificate program at the local community college.

But each morning she would come to the breakfast table with an empty look and no resolve. She missed her friends back in Hitchcock. We were living in a small neighborhood in a Boston suburb, and it was nothing like The Knoll of Hitchcock.

I finally had to admit that the plans we were discussing were really my plans, not hers. I felt if she got some training beyond her high school diploma, and a good job, I would be fulfilling my promise to Dad.

By the end of the third week, we packed up her stuff and moved her into my aunt Marie's apartment back on The Knoll of Hitchcock.

Her three oldest daughters had gotten married and left empty beds. Hannah unpacked her bags and settled in for another attempt at a future. It was during that time that my suspicion of her sleepwalking was confirmed. Great. Something else to worry about. I still hated Ma. Maybe I should have put an ad in the newspaper. *Teenage orphan – needs mother.* I wonder if she would have responded. Probably not.

CHAPTER ELEVEN

It landed on the kitchen windowsill the same time every morning. I told Mike I thought that fly was my Dad reincarnated. Maybe I was going a little crazy, but it did seem strange that a fly would follow me around for days just after I lost Dad. Six weeks had passed before we felt things were getting back to normal. The fly left finally two weeks after Hannah went back to Hitchcock.

Of course, I didn't really have a gauge for normal. I had a sister living with an aunt because our mother was still A.W.O.L, and I was probably the only twenty-five-year-old matriarch in the country.

Mike and I wanted to invite all of my relatives who helped us during my father's illness and final days to a cookout at our house in Framingham. The responses to our invitations totaled forty. The neighbors were surprised at the street full of cars when they all arrived that Sunday in October.

My surprise came two days earlier, when Mike returned from work that Friday and told me that his boss asked him to move to San Diego to open a new manufacturing plant to add to their expansion. We had to give them an answer by Monday morning.

"Mike, what about Hannah? I promised my father I would look after her. I won't be able to see a lot from three thousand miles away," I said. I could feel the tears all the way down in my chest.

Mike had been rising fast in the company and this would give him a shot at a vice-presidential slot sooner than anyone had predicted. But there was no way we could honor that request. What a weekend to have to deal with such a life-changing decision.

I was putting the final touches on the buffet table with the side dishes for the cookout on Sunday morning when I saw Hannah pulling up in our driveway with her boyfriend. I don't think I even thought about her with a boyfriend until that moment. We were a little surprised that she was nearly two hours early. But we soon discovered that was part of her plan.

"I wanted to arrive before the crowd so we could talk," she said. Her boyfriend, Joey, didn't say a word. He just let her do all the talking. She started and stopped several times as she went into all the reasons she felt it was best, until she said her final words, "Joey and I are getting married. I want to start a new life of my own."

Could this really be happening, I wondered. Maybe getting married and starting a family would be a fresh start for her, but we felt that because her boyfriend was a year younger than Hannah and still in high school, she would be starting a new life at a great disadvantage.

Where would they live? How could they survive? Dad must be rolling over in his grave ready to shoot darts at my neck. I don't suppose he expected me to interject my thoughts about future goals into her everyday life. Still, I knew he was disappointed in me.

We somehow got through the afternoon gathering and gave the appropriate thank you toasts to all the deserving relatives.

Hannah's news was never announced that day.

After everyone left that night, Mike and I decided we would accept the job offer in San Diego. Not until January. That would give us two and a half months to sell our house, plan a wedding – one for Hannah this time - and move across the country.

The next two months flew by. Keeping the house in order for showings was the most difficult. Our two babies didn't understand what 'keep your toys picked up' meant.

I was hoping that my aunt would help with a shower for Hannah. But she was not willing to support her niece who wanted to start her married life so young. It didn't even matter that she was Hannah's godmother. Or maybe it did. So, I planned and ran a bridal shower. I was her only attendant. I guess I was referred to as her matron of honor.

The mother-of-the-bride role was the one I had trouble with again this time. Once more there was no evidence that Ma was circling. I didn't hate her any less while prepping for that wedding, than I did for Connie's. In fact, maybe a little more. This was her baby getting married. I thought maybe the engagement announcement in the paper would make her sit up and take notice. Remember, Hannah was eighteen.

Girls on The Knoll of Hitchcock in 1968 were considered old maids if they weren't married by the time they were twenty-five. But she had a way to go. Her age had nothing to do with her decision.

Even that didn't bring Ma out of hiding. There had to be more than an alcohol problem. What could really be wrong with her, I wondered. Her abandonment stand had gone on too long. Was she dying? Was she seeing him again? Maybe she moved nearer to his new parish. How was she surviving? I couldn't imagine and I'm not sure I really cared. It was just hard to see another sister move through that passage in life without a mother at her side.

On December 7, 1968, I stood at the altar next to my sister as she promised to love, honor, and obey the eighteen-year-old boy on her other side. His mother cried as they walked out of the church as a married couple.

I just felt numb. It was strange calling Hannah Mrs. Joseph Jackson. The last six months had not left me with much feeling one way or the other. Maybe I should get some of those pills again, I thought. We had moved four times since Dr. Daniels told me to get out of the house before I had a nervous breakdown. I wasn't sure she was even practicing medicine anymore. And, who had time to find a new primary care physician. I sure didn't want to get whatever Ma had. She did have the fear that I might.

Over the next three weeks, we packed up our house, and wrapped the rest of our Christmas presents.

It was not a good time to get the flu, but I did. Back then no one got anything called a flu shot. At least no one I knew.

The movers were scheduled to arrive on the twenty-second and promised they would finish so that we would be at Mike's parents' house by Christmas Eve. The company sent us first class. They paid for movers to come into our house and pack our belongings.

The problem was if you didn't stay close to all three packers, they would wrap everything in sight. They packed flour left in the canisters, sugar in opened boxes from the pantry and stuffed bottles of soda in with lampshades. The mess from exploded liquid on lampshades and crawling worms in the flour and sugar took several days to correct when we finally unpacked four months later. So much for first class.

Christmas at the Moriarty's was uneventful. The snow fell as usual, and presents were exchanged. Mike and I had stopped going to church when we were out of town because they had no children's crying room in the church like the girls were used to back in Framingham. I really wanted to attended midnight mass, but my lingering fever and cough from the flu would prevent those around me from concentrating on the real reason they attended the service.

Mike's mom had her usual Manhattan after preparing

the Christmas dinner and right on cue she told me how she never liked me. I don't think she knew what she was saying when those Manhattans took full effect. She never said those things when she and Mike's dad drank beer after dinner on any other night. It happened only on holidays after she had baked and powdered her famous mincemeat squares. It became part of the holiday tradition – make the dinner, place it on the table, tell Trisha you don't like her – for as many years as I can remember. We would sometimes take bets on how long after putting the dinner on the table and the Manhattan to her lips it would take before the words were released.

But she was always there for us whenever we needed anything. Compared to Ma she was an angel. What were one or two insults a year?

Two days later we were on the road. The Dodge was packed full. The girls' toys from Christmas were piled on the floor behind the driver and passenger all the way up to the seat level.

With both girls in car seats, no one needed that space for legs. Our hope was to complete the trip before the first week in January. But there was no Beverly Hillbillies transition for us into life on the west coast.

CHAPTER TWELVE

The road south out of Massachusetts was icy because of the dropping temperatures. The back seat of our car looked like the girls' toy room in our old house. It seemed funny saying our old house. But I knew there would be a new one soon.

The girls needed to be let out of the car at regular intervals. We always took a morning break so they could run around, and I could change Erin's diaper. Then there was the stop for lunch. On most days, because the girls took a nap, we were able to drive until about four in the afternoon when we found a hotel and packed it in for the night.

Mike would get out of the car and put on his jacket, which was hanging on the hook behind his seat. It took less than a minute for me to spot a lollipop or three stuck to the back of the jacket as he was about to walk into the reception area of the hotel for the night. We used whatever method possible to keep the girls quiet on the long ride. We weren't averse to sugar bribes.

The plan was to head south from Massachusetts to Atlanta and take a right. For the most part, we followed that until we ran into an ice storm just before we got to Georgia.

By the third day of the trip, we got lost in Birmingham, Alabama. It was not a good idea to get lost in Birmingham in 1968. Everyone warned us about watching where we stopped at night. Things were quite unsettled. Martin Luther King had just been murdered. George Wallace was causing a lot of unrest, especially with his pro-segregation policies and his refusal to allow African Americans to enroll in the University. We just wanted to get to San Diego without incident. We drove on.

Spending New Year's Eve in Abilene, Texas was never on my bucket list, but it's now in my checked and done column. The girls were about as good as we could have hoped for.

Maura had a meltdown in that popular Texas town. When the waitress brought her food, she cried that she didn't want, nor had she ordered that tree on her plate.

I never did dress their servings with parsley, but I guess the restaurant was a little fancier than my dinner table back home.

Her mood moved downhill fast when she looked up from her meal to see a tall man wearing a cowboy hat and carrying a gun in a holster. I think it was the first time she ever saw one up close. Mister Rogers never addressed cowboys on his wonderful-day-in-the-neighborhood offerings. She spent the rest of the night sitting up in bed staring at the hotel room door making sure that man didn't come to get her. I think it was the longest night of the trip.

It took us seven days to get to the west coast. Driving through Texas seemed like forever. I never saw so much tumbleweed.

The Arizona dessert was a little frightening because we couldn't see an end. The climb over the mountains to get to California was beautiful. It made you forget any unpleasantness in your life.

Stopping that last night, which would be the first night of the rest of our lives, was especially rewarding. The views were spectacular whichever way you looked.

Harbor and Shelter Islands were dotted with palm trees and flowers spreading between the water and the upscale hotels. And, from Mission Bay you only saw acres of sail until the water met the tip of Coronado Island.

We decided to take a room on Pacific Beach. It would be a hoot to call our friends back home and tell them about building sandcastles while they were shoveling snow. It didn't quite turn out as we planned.

After buying a two-seater stroller so I could go for walks in the morning along the beautiful palm-lined walkways to the shops a few blocks away, I only got to use it twice. It rained non-stop.

We found a housing development in a town called University City. It was just east of LaJolla, and was a new area that was considered to be the most up and coming town in Southern California. The entire area was made up of hills and valleys. We found a brand new development and bought a house scheduled to be ready in six weeks.

By the end of the next week, we had four more inches of rain. The wait for our new house was pushed back two weeks longer. The weathermen were all amazed at the most unusual weather in southern California. It rained for an entire month. The result was four more weeks to wait for the house completion. I would have built an ark if I had a way to get the wood.

The suite we were staying in had two bedrooms. The girls shared one room with a crib for Erin while Maura slept on a big girl's bed. It was big enough for Goldilocks and all the bears in the forest. The only advantage was we never had to worry about her falling out.

During the day I would put Erin in her crib for a nap and then bring Maura into our bedroom and read to her until she fell off to sleep. It was the rest of the day that gave me pause and exacerbated my cabin fever.

I didn't know anyone in the area and missed my friends back in Massachusetts. The only person I talked to regularly was the hotel operator, Marcia. Back then, you had to go through the operator any time you had to make a call. She would ask how the girls were getting along and we would have a real girlie conversation.

One afternoon, during the second month of our stay,

Erin woke up from her nap with a temperature of one hundred and six. I was always under the impression that anything over one hundred and four caused death. I called Marcia in a panic. I had no idea where the nearest hospital was located. Besides, Mike had our car at the plant, and I didn't have a pediatrician lined up yet. Marcia sent up ice for the bathtub and extra towels to try to get Erin's fever down.

I wished I could talk to my mother for advice. Where would I call? Information had no listing for Ma in Hitchcock. It was the only place I could try. By then she was probably miles away. I actually thought of trying to reach Father Fitz just to see if he had any current information about Ma. But I didn't really know where he was either. Again, Ma was not reachable.

Mike arrived in time to help with the alcohol rub on Erin's arms that brought her temp down to one hundred and four. Not a good place, but a much safer one than before. We decided to take her to the hospital anyway, because we needed to find her some medicine in case the temperature spiked during the night.

That was how I met Dr. Buck, a lovely old man with a Parkinson's shake to his hands. He thought she had picked up a virus and felt Maura would probably come down with whatever it was soon. I could hardly wait. We were spared that fate, but not the housing completion disaster.

Even though everyone we spoke with talked about the most unusual weather in San Diego, we felt a black cloud had been following us for months. From Christmas to Easter, we spent in hotel rooms trying to keep our sanity. At least Mike got to go to work and talk with grown-ups. My language began to sound a little elementary. Miss Jean from Romper Room was the only adult I heard from on a daily basis. The real rip was taking care of Erin. Her fever left quickly but she broke out with boils from her waist down to her thighs. Every visit to Dr. Buck's gave us another possibility to consider for the cause. The one requirement was to keep those sores as exposed to the air as possible.

Imagine the challenge of keeping a toddler who was in diapers from wetting any of her surroundings, without the benefit of rubber pants. Back then we did not have anything called Pampers. Cloth diapers were the norm. Different pastel colored rubber pants completed the ensemble and became a required part of the regular undergarment wardrobe. The instructions were to take off her rubber pants and allow her sores to become more exposed to the air. Remember we were staying at hotels. Following her around and making sure there were no permanent stains on furniture or carpeting kept me more than occupied.

Finally, we were referred to the doctors at the Salk Institute in LaJolla. They found the cure for polio; maybe a little rash on a toddler could be diagnosed without much effort on their part.

The next few months flew by. Regular visits to the Institute with Erin brought the diagnosis of a staph infection. The doctors felt she must have picked it up during our trip across the country. Go figure. What it meant was that she would need injections twice each week under the first layer of skin, but not into the second. Picture that needle going into her little arm.

For the first two months, the Salk doctors administered the shots. However, after they saw there was improvement, the treatment was entrusted to the shaky hands of Dr. Buck. God help us. The success was dependent on the accuracy and frequency. We could assure the frequency – the accuracy was always the challenge.

The move into our new house was like winning the lottery. Our furniture was delivered, and it felt like new because we hadn't seen it for five months. There were several days of unpacking and finding new locations for treasured belongings. The lampshades that were stained from the coke that exploded out of the bottles that were packed in the same box had to be replaced. We also decided to deep six the canisters that traveled across the country and spent several months in storage. The packers didn't think emptying them out before packing would cause problems. The crawling creatures among the flour and sugar proved otherwise.

Living at the top of a canyon with snakes in the gutters was a new experience for the family. We were kept busy laying in a new patio and building a retaining wall in the backyard. Snails were prevalent in the area and Maura adopted one immediately.

She called it Shelly. She was always very literal.

Soon after settling in, we got the call to say that Hannah delivered a baby boy. They named him James Robert. His middle name was chosen after Dad. He would have loved a grandson. I'm sure Hannah would have appreciated the advice and help of a mother at the time. She was going it alone, again. They say what doesn't kill you makes you stronger. She must have been made of steel by that time.

Spending any holiday in California turned into a new experience for east coast transplants. Everything happened outdoors. The houses were over the top with decorations. The neighborhood streets lit up like fireworks on the fourth of July. I even joined in the California way of celebrating by putting blue lights on our Christmas tree.

Progressive dinners were a new concept for us and a regular weekly gathering at neighbors' houses was a welcome pattern.

Spring was even better. There were the occasional drawbacks. The morning we were thrown out of bed at dawn was our introduction to earthquakes. After we got accustomed to the jingle of cups and saucers rattling from time to time and watching our picture window rolling sideways in motions resembling waves at sea, life in the land of milk and honey was a piece of cake.

We got involved in clubs and organizations and San Diego seemed like wonderland. Mike's stock was rising in the company, and I finally felt like a California housewife. Forming a local chapter of the Newcomers Club kept me busy and allowed me to meet new friends.

At the end of March, Hannah called to say that her husband had joined the Marines and was stationed at Camp Pendleton for boot camp. Because it was only a short ride north from San Diego, she was planning to fly to our house with Jimmy and see Joey before he was shipped to Guam at the end of April. It would be good to see her and, of course my new nephew.

"Ma's in the hospital," were the first words I heard when I picked up the phone two weeks later. It was Hannah's voice. "The doctors don't know what's wrong. They're taking tests," she informed me.

"Holy shit," I replied. "How did you find out? What hospital is she in?" I couldn't believe what I was hearing. Not that Ma was sick enough to be in a hospital, but that Hannah would know about it, was unbelievable.

"She called me last night and asked for help," Hannah continued. I followed the ambulance and spoke with the admitting doctor."

"Were you as shocked as I am to hear she was still living," I asked.

"Not really. She sent me a card when I was in the hospital when Jimmy was born. She moved back into the area and wanted to see the baby," she said. "I was going to tell you about it when I came to visit next week" she added.

I guess maybe I should have had sons instead of daughters, I thought. "What does it look like" I asked.

"They think it's her liver, but they won't know for sure until they get the results of the tests," she said. "Her skin is yellow, and her stomach looks pretty bloated. I'll call you tomorrow when I know more."

I didn't sleep very well that night. Ma was still alive.

Well, at least for now. I was sure her liver was damaged. No one could put that much alcohol into their body and not have a liver problem. Maybe now Hannah would have the relationship that she missed growing up. Missing her wedding was one thing, but maybe helping her raise her son would make up for some of that lost bonding.

Maybe now Ma would also get help for that sickness she talked about when I saw her. The one she hoped I would never get. I might even find out it was something I could get tested for and ensure it never happened to me.

The phone woke us up early. It was still dark outside.

"Ma died," Hannah whispered so low I wasn't sure if I was dreaming or listening to my sister on the other end of the line.

"Are you all right," I asked.

"Yes," she said. "They confirmed cirrhosis of the liver and added several other meaningless medical terms to their report when they gave us the news. Connie is taking care of things at the hospital," she said with a voice that concerned me, "I think the funeral home arrangements will be finalized by the end of the day."

I dropped the girls off at day care and spent the morning walking the beach. Most women would be packing for the trip to their mother's funeral. I was frozen in place. Looking out at the ocean I thought of all the times I wanted to tell Ma how I felt. Now it would never happen. It would be hypocritical to rush to her coffin. I had two sisters back there who could handle the arrangements. It was less than twenty months since I had completed those tasks for Dad's funeral. To stand in a receiving line listening to what people might want to say about our mother was not something I needed to hear. I had listened to what people said about Ma for enough years to hold me 'till the next life.

I didn't go.

It felt so strange going through the motions of that day in my life. The visualization of them putting her in the ground gave me the chills. I would hear all the details when Hannah got to San Diego on Saturday.

The airport was crowded that weekend when Hannah stepped off the plane with my nephew. He had tested her stability from the moment they turned off the fasten-your-seatbelt sign until their decent into the San Diego airport. It had been a little more than twenty-four hours since she buried our mother. She definitely needed a few days with her husband at Camp Pendleton. He would be preparing for his tour in Guam, but a little R&R would be good for them both.

We spent the afternoon catching up with the details of Ma's re-entry into Hannah's life. Mike enjoyed having a little boy in the house after being outnumbered for so long. And I was introduced to the joys of changing a diaper on a baby who could squirt you with urine while still laying in the diaper-changing position. By the end of the week, I was a pro. It was nice being able to let Hannah enjoy time with her husband.

I found it difficult watching her get back on that plane a few days later. It was uncertain how long it would be before we saw each other again.

She looked happy for the first time in years. I was relieved. Maybe things could work out well for them. It was wonderful seeing her as a mother.

Her son seemed like such a happy baby. Hannah's married life seemed all that she had wanted. Maybe Dad wouldn't be upset with me after all. And, with Ma gone, maybe we could both go on with our lives like other normal wives and mothers. We had no idea as we waved goodbye to one another that the most shocking of our mother's secrets was yet to be revealed.

CHAPTER THIRTEEN

The Pink Panther drove us up the canyon and into our University City neighborhood. It was the name the girls gave my five-year-old pink Nash Rambler. They thought of it as one of their larger toys - the one that their mom drove.

It normally took us up and down the canyons of University City and LaJolla like our own personal roller coaster on wheels. My third pregnancy caused more than a need for bedroom reassignments. In my third trimester, it was harder for me to drive because my pregnant stomach hung through the opening of the steering wheel and prevented me from turning the wheel. The only solution was to push my seat back far enough to allow a couple of inches between my belly button and the steering wheel. But then my feet didn't reach the pedals, making it nearly impossible for me to move forward or backward. In other words – drive the car. Mike had to cut wooden blocks and attach them to the foot pedals with metal brackets so that I could reach them with the seat that far back.

I hadn't planned to be pregnant that year. It was a total surprise - so much for the rhythm method. We were just starting to enjoy our California lifestyle. One of our favorite hangouts was Old Town. I don't think it was because the Mexican food was exceptional, although we hadn't found much that could compare. It was the atmosphere that kept us going back on a regular basis.

No matter where we went, we felt like it was a little glimpse of paradise. The palm trees and warm breezes from the Mexican border all the way up to Rancho Bernardo, half-way to Los Angeles, offered us acres of the playground we now found ourselves enjoying. Women shopping for groceries at two in the morning in their nightgowns did give us pause. Just being able to stop at a store for a forgotten gallon of milk for breakfast on our way home from an evening at the theatre was new to us.

Our former life was but a memory. There was no snow, no ice and after the first few months in California, very little rain. Their Santa Anna winds were the only weather-related concerns people talked about. That's because the nearly forty mile an hour winds brought the warm air from the desert, causing the fear of fires, especially during long periods of drought.

Maura and Erin were in pre-school classes at the nursery school and my best friend, Rosemary and I used that time to learn new crafts, shop at the malls and attend the many activities of the Newcomers Club that I formed during my house-waiting days.

Many of my peers across the country in the seventies were flower children. They smoked pot and wore colorful beads that didn't necessarily match the rest of their clothing. I never had that luxury, or even the desire for that matter, to join them.

The California fashions for the rest of us included wearing hot pants and boots. I loved those white boots. They made me feel like I was part of the "In" crowd. With those boots on even a girl from The Knoll could pass as one of the new generation of Californians.

It was a time in our history when men wore their hair down to or below their shoulders and the Rolling Stones played on all our car radios. It seemed like people were more fit and healthy before the McDonald's era.

Neighborhood parties were also prevalent and there were several activities that shocked my New England roots.

The forever-to-be-remembered pool party at one of the neighbors was among the shockers. The owner was a clothing designer and had just created the one-piece pantsuit for men. He modeled it as soon as the majority of the invited guests arrived. Rosemary and I were looking through the color options in one of his many overstuffed closets when we heard everyone yelling out back. It forced us toward the noise outdoors and poolside.

There was a pile of keys on the floor of the patio. All the men at the party placed their keys in the pile and took turns picking up a set that belonged to someone else. The idea was that the keys allowed the man entry into the home of someone else's wife. What happened after that was left to one's imagination. Rosemary and I were furious and left the party. We wanted no part of the humiliation.

We rode around town until we felt our husbands had gotten the idea, we were not going to play that game. Not long after that night I discovered I was pregnant. Maybe I should have let Mike take someone else's keys.

Shannon was born on April 14th. The doctor took an extremely long time to get to the hospital requiring the nurses to keep my final pushing far at bay. My obstetrician said he stalled on purpose because I wouldn't want a child born on the thirteenth. I think he was just trying to finish his evening out with friends.

This third child of ours did not arrive with blonde fuzz like her older sisters. She was born with flaming red hair. Rosemary's husband Bud was a redhead, and we took a lot of razzing from our neighbors for several months after her birth. Rosemary and Bud agreed to be godparents for Shannon. They were our closest friends, and we thought they would be in our lives forever.

That fall Maura started kindergarten. The elementary school was across a major four-lane street that ran the length of University City, about five blocks from the house where we lived. There were no buses assigned to our section of town.

The students living in the area just walked together up to the fifth-grade crossing guard and, after he stopped all the oncoming traffic, they were allowed to cross.

I thought I would die before I'd let my little girl go with the neighborhood children on that walk. Even though she was the den mother of the nursery when she was born, she was still my little girl - emphasis on little. But there was no other option.

What I never told her was that for the first month, I put Erin and Shannon in the Pink Panther right after Maura left the house. We drove in the crawl mode while she and the neighborhood kids met the crossing guard. Then we just sat idling until she got to the other side of the major highway and the front entrance of the school.

Just when I got to the stage where I might let her go one morning without following a street behind, my world was jolted one more time. A seismic shift in my world was about to occur. The word came without warning.

Shannon was seven months old and was finally settling into a routine of regular sleeping and eating hours. There were even kitchen-table-talks about putting her into a daycare facility two mornings each week. I'd be able to use those hours to get things done that were impossible to handle with a baby to watch.

"I was told that I'm needed back in Massachusetts," Mike said in between bites of his morning croissant.

"Not yet. The kids are too little. We're just getting settled and have so much more to see and do in California," I replied. "Couldn't you consider looking for a job out here," I pleaded.

But there was not much movement on his part. Or on

his company's part. I was not happy to hear about their decision. We were forced to leave this lifestyle and return to Massachusetts, if Mike wanted to remain with his company. They needed him back east.

I really wanted to stay in California. We had settled into a way of life that kept us happy. There was nothing good drawing me back to Massachusetts. I had bad memories of my last years there and we had certainly become accustomed to the wonderful weather we enjoyed in California.

But, after trying to convince Mike that he should apply for jobs in the San Diego area, there was little choice but to agree to the company's new requirement. We put the house up for sale and started packing. As it turned out, the house didn't sell in time for our move, so the company bought it from us and eventually sold it.

Before we set out on this three-thousand-mile trip with three kids, we bought a brand-new station wagon with dual-facing rear seats. There was a table that would rise in the middle. Maura and Erin spent a good part of each day coloring and drawing on that table. Shannon was in her car seat in the second seat behind Mike so I could tend to her needs as we drove.

I spent many miles in the second seat myself being pulled between the crayons behind me and the necessary diaper changes and scratch and sniff books to my left.

The return trip was similar to our trip out to California four years earlier with the exception of one more child and the fact that we took a slightly different route back. It allowed us to spend a night in Texarkana.

Can you imagine sitting in a restaurant on the corner of Texas and Arkansas? The town got its name when a surveyor came to the Texas state line and nailed a board to a tree. It came from TEXas, ARKansas and LouisiANA, which was believed to be only a few miles to the south. It was actually thirty miles away, but the name stuck. It was certainly a strange experience. I took a picture with one foot in Texas and one in Arkansas.

Arriving back in Massachusetts in January was probably not the best timing for our spirits. The snow was falling, and I just shivered for the first few weeks until my body got acclimated to the new temperature. Anytime I phoned Rosemary in San Diego she would remind me of the sunny and warm weather in her backyard. She was sure we would be returning soon. She didn't understand why we left.

I had no reassuring explanation because I didn't understand completely why we left.

The first place we looked for housing when we returned to Massachusetts was our old stomping grounds in Framingham. After just a week of working with a realtor, we purchased a garrison colonial in a new development called Pheasant Hill and were able to move into the just completed dwelling in a matter of a few weeks. With the needs of three children there could be no repeat of the infamous California waiting period.

The neighborhood was comprised of mostly Jewish residents. We soon got into a rhythm of going to someone's Bar Mitzvah if it was a neighbor's son, or Bat Mitzvah if it was a neighbor's daughter. When other children moved on our street, my daughters would ask, "Are you Christmas or Hanukkah?" They preferred the latter because they thought getting presents for eight nights instead of one would bring them a greater haul.

The houses were large and sat high on a hill. There were actually pheasants on that hill when we first moved there. Within a few short months, Mike and I became very active in our new surroundings, eventually agreeing to serve as co-chairs of our neighborhood civic association.

While there were some responsibilities for town affairs, the position primarily consisted of being in charge of all the regular social activities of the neighborhood.

Bridge was popular with most of the couples and the annual parade with original floats made and decorated by each family turned out to be the favorite of adults and children alike.

I missed my lifestyle back in San Diego but tried to bury myself in my new suburban one just a half hour west of Boston. Most of the activities enjoyed by the wives of the area included babysitting in the price. I played on the tennis team, attended the weekly Mah Jong games each Tuesday and shopped 'til I dropped. There were some advantages of my husband's new job. Eventually I became known as the only non-Jewish American Princess in the neighborhood. I finally got to a position in life that most women would die for. But I was not a happy camper.

Then it came to me. I needed to close some doors. Coming east brought back all the memories I left in Massachusetts four years earlier. It was time to visit Ma's grave. I hired a babysitter and drove to Hitchcock.

My first stop was the Rectory at the St. Mary's parish so that I could find out exactly where Ma was buried. The housekeeper took me into a room with lots of bookcases as well as a long conference table with several chairs. She brought me a couple of books with records of parishioners and their vital statistics. I was sure I had found the wrong information and called her in to confirm my belief. She assured me that I was looking at accurate documents. How could that be? The records stated that Ma had two brothers. But Ma said she was an only child. Who were these brothers? My stomach moved up and down inside my body. I asked to see the priest on duty.

He confirmed that the records were accurate, but he didn't have any information other than their names - Thomas and John. John was deceased, but Thomas was still living. I felt faint.

My next stop was to visit with Granny. She had moved off of The Knoll along with so many other former residents. Puerto Rican migrant farm workers, attracted by jobs in Western Massachusetts, began moving into one apartment after another in the tenements formerly occupied by the original Irish and French residents. Some of the new immigrants, not willing to wait for apartments to empty, even started fires to encourage people to move out. The arson years of the seventies destroyed over three thousand apartments on The Knoll. For the first time in my life, I heard prejudiced remarks out of the mouths of my relatives. They now referred to the new neighbors as "those PR's."

My aunt and uncle lived in the apartment next door to Granny for as long as I could remember. They knew it was time to get off The Knoll and they found a house in Chicopee. They couldn't leave Granny and her-physically challenged daughter, my aunt Wilma. So, they invited them to move into their new house.

Because Wilma only walked by holding on and pushing the back of a small chair, and wouldn't be able to handle stairs, my aunt and uncle decided to let Granny and Wilma live on the main floor of their three-bedroom ranch house and they would finish the basement and live downstairs. I'm sure they didn't imagine that Granny would live well into her nineties when they made that decision.

When I called Granny to say I was coming to visit she insisted I come for lunch. At this point in her life, she wasn't eating the large meals we all remembered from our childhood. She would make a sandwich and cut it into fours. Then place each quarter of that sandwich on a plate.

She would then add a cup of soup to each meal she served. It was a good start on a weight-loss program, I reasoned.

She was still wearing those cotton housedresses and the same black two-inch block high-heeled shoes - the ones the nuns wore. I did notice that she seemed to walk a little slower. She told me that my cousins took turns driving her to the store each week to replenish her supply of soup and anything else she had a fancy for. She had a habit of clicking her tongue on the upper part of her mouth and making a "tsk" sound. She did it more when she didn't like something and wanted to show her displeasure.

When we finished lunch, Wilma went back into her room to write some letters and I sat with Granny in her kitchen. It was hard beginning the conversation, but I was sure she had to know something about these uncles of mine, maybe even why Ma or Dad didn't tell us anything about them.

My conversation with Granny was different from any other I ever had with her. She was very surprised that I had this information. To say she was reluctant would be an understatement.

"Why do you want to open such a door" she wanted to know. Ma and Dad were both dead and there was no one else to ask.

"Why was it necessary for it to take this long to open the door?" I asked. She had no answer for that question.

"Yes, there were two brothers" she began. "The younger one committed suicide when he was just a teenager" she continued.

My face started burning from my neck upward. I didn't expect to hear those words.

"I believe your mother's older brother was sent to some mental institution out of town."

My ears were now burning. I couldn't believe what I was hearing – an insane asylum? Two uncles - each with some kind of mental problem. Was Ma suffering from something similar? Could that be what she meant when she told me she hoped I was never sick like she was? Is that why she became an alcoholic? Is that why Dad never divorced her, even though she left him to fend for himself when he became ill? So many questions.

"Is there anything else I might find out in my new quest to learn about Ma's family," I asked.

"There were lots of rumors when her father died," she said. "Some busy bodies were saying he never fell down those stairs to his death at all, but she pushed him."

"Who pushed him?"

She was looking out the window when she finally said, "Your grandmother."

I drove back to Framingham in a trance. I went through the motions, but never knew how I got the eighty miles down the Massachusetts Turnpike. My mother had a secret family. How could she have kept that secret from us all those years?

Did she really feel we would turn our backs on her brother? As soon as I finished one question another one came to mind. There was so much I never knew about my mother. Things began to make more sense than ever before. But, then more questions.

Could she have been going to Father Fitz for counseling? Did he take advantage of her weak state?

Was there blood when her brother committed suicide? Could that be why she fainted at the sight of blood?

Was she at home when her father died at the bottom of those stairs?

Did she see someone push him?

Was that why they put her brother away?

I would never know for sure. I needed to find out more about my uncles. Maybe something would make sense. I made one decision that night. If it took the rest of my life, I would get answers.

CHAPTER FOURTEEN

It has been over thirty years since that afternoon in Granny's kitchen when I found out about Ma's secret family.

Granny has since passed away. Only a few months shy of making it onto one of the *Today Show* jelly jars of centurions. She was probably one of my greatest losses. She really was like a mother to me. Bringing my three daughters to view the woman who guided me through my formative years was like coming full circle.

After the initial shock, I accepted the fact that Ma probably was ashamed of coming from a family with mental illness. I was reminded of how she married into a family that was placed high on the list of respected ones from her birthplace. Back then people kept many illnesses secret.

My father's sister, Wilma was partially paralyzed from the waist down. I saw pictures of her when she could walk.

Everyone said she fell over the threshold and became crippled. We all believed that story. To this day, I've never had a conversation with anyone about the real cause of her paralysis. I watched her pull herself up to a standing position, lean on a small chair and push it while dragging her feet one at a time. She had enough strength to hold her in that standing position but couldn't let go of the chair or she would be on the ground.

Dad had another sister, Helen, who died of breast cancer. Back then no one used the word cancer. They used to refer to anyone who had cancer as someone with the big C. In fact, my father's generation never discussed any weakness in any part of their bodies from the neck to the knees. I guess those things were sacred.

Mental illness was a different animal altogether. You were just called crazy. Ma must have been ashamed to admit that she grew up around anyone with this kind of affliction. I began to believe mental illness was what she was trying not to tell me about, back in her apartment that day on Acorn Street.

After Granny died, I tried to find out more about my mother's childhood years growing up on The Knoll, only three blocks away from the Newton family. Dad's sister,

Marie, who was also my mother's former classmate, helped me refine my quest.

My research into Ma's real life as a child brought only sketchy information. I did learn that she was just twelve years old when her father, Edward fell - or was pushed - down those stairs. I'll never know if she was at home when it happened. Or whether her mother had anything to do with his death?

I wondered what it was like living in a house with an alcoholic father. Then I remembered that I lived in a house with an alcoholic mother. Was there a real difference? He might have been more difficult to ignore. The societal description of an Irishman with a liking for the sauce has always been that of a drunk. He did manage to hold down a regular job. In fact, he was a foreman at the American Whiting Paper Mill. A job that men from the neighborhood looked up to at the time.

The well-respected shop was known as Frasier No. 2, a subsidiary of the largest shoe manufactory in the world. Its' parent company was based in Aberdeen, Scotland. The Hitchcock factory was located on Sycamore St. at the corner of Linden St. Everyone called the office building, "The Flat Iron" because its shape resembled a household iron.

After contacting the Massachusetts Department of Developmental Services, I learned that Ma's oldest brother, Thomas, was committed to the Belchertown State School on October 2, 1933 - the same year Ma's father died. Could my uncle Thomas have been involved in his father's death? Maybe that was why they sent him away after caring for him at home for eighteen years.

Two years later, when her brother John committed suicide at sixteen, Ma was only fourteen. I can't help wondering if she saw him before they took him away, or if it happened in the house. Could she have been the one who found him? Was there a lot of blood? The questions don't stop. Her fear of blood and any medical professionals could have stemmed from her experiences at home during what must have been unbearable to accept.

According to the city census records, she lived in that same apartment for five more years. That was when she and her mother reportedly moved to North Walnut Street. That same year she became engaged to my dad.

There is no question in my mind now that Dad knew about her brother, more likely both brothers.

He could have even been involved with her decision to

keep Thomas' existence a secret. I'm sure she was afraid that people might think less of her because of her bloodline. The fact that he never divorced her may not have only been because of his religious upbringing.

When my uncle Thomas was committed to the Belchertown State School, he was no longer a boy. Yet, they were all called boys and girls and their adult wards were decorated with cartoon characters, similar to pediatric units in hospital rooms.

I think anyone who had any affliction out of the ordinary was put away in those days. People were misdiagnosed all the time. I am still not sure what the diagnosis was that accounted for my uncle Thomas' admittance into the facility. The fact that it was called the School for the Feeble Minded gives me some indication to reason that he wasn't there because he was gifted. The records are scarce because the school was closed for good at the time of my research.

The name they gave the place my uncle Thomas lived in for most of his life threw me for a loop - The Belchertown State School for the Feeble-Minded.

Several studies during the twenties and thirties resulted in the development of a system of classification based on

IQ. Anyone scoring below ninety was labeled downhill from dullness to morons, to imbeciles and finally idiots. The more common name given to anyone with intellectual disabilities was feeble-minded. The legal records at the Belchertown State School referred to more than half of the fifteen hundred residents as idiots.

The school itself was situated on over six hundred acres of land just a short distance outside of Hitchcock on farmland. It would have been so easy to visit him often if we had only been told he was there. A group of family members formed "The Friends" and met just like a PTA during the fifties. We were never part of that group. We could have been if we knew it existed.

When the building was completed, the main campus included the original farm that provided produce to the residents, eleven dormitories, an infirmary and nine cottages for employees. According to a January 1945 article in the *Belchertown Sentinel*, An Afternoon at the State Farm, "...the original farm grew to 225 acres by World War II. The finished physical plant included two farm dormitories, two horse barns, two dairy barns, a large cow hospital, a greenhouse, a poultry plant, and a piggery.

The farm was its own self-contained community within

the larger, self-contained community of the school. It produced all of the school's milk and potatoes, most of its other winter vegetables and eggs, and a substantial amount of chicken, pork and beef."

The dormitories housed either boys or girls. The only time they were in the same building was to eat. They would continue to be called boys and girls well into their eighties and unfortunately would be treated like children.

In her book - *I Raise My Eyes to Say Yes* - Ruth Sienkiewicz describes the eight wards on two floors referred to as the infirmary. "The females were housed in wards one through four on the first floor and the males were on the second floor in wards five through eight. About half the people on ward four talked to themselves, mumbling semi-intelligible comments to nobody in particular. Usually, three or four radios were blaring away at any given time. On a loud day, all of the noises on the ward combined to create a truly maddening din."

Ruth moved into the Belchertown infirmary before her twelfth birthday and remained at the institution until she moved into a state supported apartment in Springfield, Massachusetts at the age of twenty-eight. She was a quad-riplegic as a result of Cerebral Palsy and was unable to speak or move any part of her body except her eyes. Eventually, with the help of the Tufts Interactive Communicator she was able to express herself and was able to author her book. She explained, "By hitting a head switch at the right moment, I could select a letter, which would then appear at the top of the grid and allow me to spell out words and even sentences."

Her frustration at being placed on a mat on the floor with six other patients without the ability to move on her own, was only one of the many ways the institution overlooked the needs of their residents.

The treatment became public in the nineties when the state was forced to close its doors as a result of the scandalous expose of the conditions and the investigation into the deaths at the school. Several accounts of the findings were published in the local newspapers, and others reported to the state offices with their findings.

The most disturbing was a six-part series, *The Tragedy of Belchertown*, written by James Shanks, a staff writer at the Springfield Union in 1970. He wrote "the smell and sight overpowered the stink."

He was referring to the men in Building K. He went on to write," but if that's bad, the sight of men – other human beings – but retarded – standing around naked or holding their pants up because the laundry ruined the fasteners, is worse."

"Physically grown men," Shanks continued, "roll on a cold tile floor, sit in grotesque positions, motionless, or rock rhythmically back and forth. Others are bent in strange poses on stark prison-made benches. About one hundred and twenty men lived in Building K. The youngest was fifteen, the oldest over eighty – mentally, all two-year-old's in the physical bodies of grown-ups. There was no privacy. They slept in large barracks, beds touching head to foot, a narrow twelve-inch aisle separating rows. Clothing and other personal effects were kept on small, open shelves in another room. There were two bathrooms, each with six toilets – no toilet seats and no partitions. A single open shower stood at one end of each lavatory.

Only three attendants," Shanks said, "cared for the men during the day and only two at night. Each day attendant was responsible for forty men - dispose of night soiling, bathe and feed the men, and send out the laundry. When the laundry returned, they had to sort and place the clothes in the appropriate man. The residents, many of them nude, sat all day on benches, or on the bare floor in strange and grotesque positions, sometimes in pools of their own waste."

There is no way of knowing whether my uncle Thomas was among those one hundred and twenty men in Building K. The article was written two years after he was transferred to Boston. I don't believe the facility could have been a stellar place to live only two years before the Shanks series.

The closest insight I have gotten into my uncle's time there is probably fed by my imagination. Doris Dickinson of Belchertown's Historical Society, before she retired to South Carolina, told Robert Hornick for his book, *The Girls and Boys of Belchertown*, about an email she received from the former head farmer at the school. In his email he a referred to a resident who worked on the farm he called T. The email stated, "*T. had no known family and only received a Christmas card once each year from someone he called his aunt. He would carry that card in his pocket until the middle of summer when you could no longer see images due to its age.*"

I would like to think he was talking about my uncle Thomas. My imagination takes me to the belief that T. was referring to my mother's, and if so his aunt Margie? I will never know. I can't be sure if my uncle was among the residents of the school who were treated badly, but there is no documentation that refers to anyone receiving good treatment at that facility.

Albert Warner was a former resident released on parole in 1937, just three years after my uncle was admitted. Before his release he worked as a mail carrier that allowed him to get around and meet other residents. After his release he worked as a house painter and eventually married another former resident. He told an interviewer that he had some good times up there and that everything wasn't so bad.

I'd like to believe my uncle's time there was as good as Warner's. He and his wife decided that the people who died in residence needed to be remembered and he visited their graves in Potters Field on the Belchertown grounds often. He was bothered by the disrepair of the graveyard and began a campaign to improve the grounds.

In 1987, the state erected a monument and listed the names of those buried there. They eventually agreed to refurbish the gravesite and install granite markers with names and dates placed on each gravestone. I walked thru the site looking at the individual stones on the ground for a marker that displayed the name of Thomas Sheehan. My uncle's name was not on that monument. He is not buried there.

After checking with the Massachusetts DDS, they could only confirm that he was transferred from Belchertown to a Boston State School on May 8, 1967. That facility has since been torn down. All I have is a document that states Thomas Edward Sheehan died in Boston on November 11, 1987. The Deputy Assistant Commissioner, Victor Hernandez, of the Massachusetts DDS continues to try to confirm where he was buried. There may be a time in the future when I could actually visit his grave.

In his book *Crimes Against Humanity*, Professor Benjamin Ricci documented his son Robert's experience as a resident of the Belchertown State School. He was concerned that residents never got outdoors for fresh air and was informed that residents are not outdoors because there isn't enough help. Keeping track of people proved difficult and some residents "vanished into thin air."

He discovered that one third of the eligible residents were denied their right to an education. The mental health bureaucrats wouldn't share sensitive information with the biological parents. Four deaths were attributed to lack of public safety. He finally formed the Advocacy Network group and through their efforts the institution was closed in December 1992.

CHAPTER FIFTEEN

If Ma was afraid of being committed like her brother, it might explain her nervous condition and could even account for the way she used and eventually abused alcohol.

If she wondered if her genes carried cells that would push her to suicide like her brother John, booze could calm some of those fears - for a time.

If she was simply trying to make sure no one ever found out about her family, leaving the area so no one could ask would be a solution she may have tried more than once.

During the time after Ma left and was living on her own, the only meeting of Alcoholics Anonymous in Western Massachusetts was held in Hitchcock. But I will never know if she ever attended a meeting.

One requirement for regular attendance would be to refrain from drinking. It's hard to remember a time when Ma wasn't drinking. That would have been one of the referral programs the parish priests would have sent a patient to if it was decided that a program like AA could be beneficial. Of course, that's assuming you went to the parish priest for help.

Could Ma have gone to Father Fitz for help? Did he offer her something else?

I do know that I never went to any Adult Children of Alcoholics meetings back then. I never found out about them until the eighties during my own time in counseling.

Two years after I went to St. Mary's rectory to look at their records, I received a package in the mail that contained the Mass book we donated to the church when Dad died. The diocese decided that the parish was not able to sustain itself with the small amount of money coming in each month. The new Puerto Rican residents were not supporting the parish.

Everything on the compound was torn down. The eight-hundred-pound bell from the tower is the only remaining part of the original Church. It is marked by a plaque and sits on the corner of a small park. A tower of senior housing and four duplex houses fill the rest of the space formerly occupied by the buildings and grounds in which so many of our lives were formed.

I did have the occasion to find myself face to face with

the Rev. Fitzroy Brennan one more time. It was 2003 and a reunion was held for anyone who had grown up on The Knoll. The diocese was closing the other Catholic Church in Ward 1. The only one left at the time. The event included a Mass and celebratory dinner to follow at a local establishment.

As the Mass began the choir sang all the familiar songs. I saw the altar boys coming down the side aisle where I had chosen to sit with my current husband and other family members. I saw that the priest following behind the altar boys had a full head of white hair, and it still sat high on his head. It could be no other. He was there to say this final Mass.

During his sermon he mentioned that he remembered his days at St. Mary's down the street. I wanted to stand up and ask if he remembered the affair with my mother, but my uncle sitting next to me, held my arm. I think he knew exactly what I was about to do.

Before continuing with the Mass, he said he would be retiring very soon, due to his health, from the parish where he was currently serving as Pastor. It was only a few towns away. How could the Roman Catholic Diocese of Springfield let him back into their territory? He had served time at a parish in the Boston area when he left Hitchcock and is reported to have had an affair with a weatherwoman in the area. There have been more recent claims by more than one woman stating she also had an affair with him while he was in Hitchcock.

Was that why Ma ran away that day I came home sick? Did she think she was the only one?

Before Father Fitz retired in 2003, he was transferred to a parish in Agawam, MA. They have an educational program through the twelfth grade, just like the one at St. Mary's. It's just forty minutes away from Hitchcock. They actually promoted him to pastor. After his retirement from Agawam, he spent some time living in a retirement home for clergy in Florida. At this writing, however, there is a record of him living in North Carolina.

The bishop in charge when we requested Father Fitz's transfer has since died, but is now under investigation himself, along with forty-six other clergy in the Springfield diocese for alleged abuse toward a total of one hundred and seventeen under-aged credible victims. There are very few records documenting affairs with subsequent transfers.

According to an Associated Press article on July 23, 2004, "The Springfield Diocese reached a proposed settlement of more than $7 million with the 46 people who accused priests of molesting them when they were children."

But the abuse by clergy has not limited itself to western Massachusetts. Also, it has not always been made known to the public. Just like the way Father Fitzroy Brennan was quietly transferred to another part of Massachusetts without information forwarded or left behind, and others in authority did the same.

The Associated Press reported in January of 2013 that retired Cardinal Roger Mahony of the largest Roman Catholic archdiocese in the United States – Los Angeles - was stripped of his administrative duties. He was required per order of the court to release thousands of pages of confidential files on sexually abusive priests. Some files that were released showed that he and other top aides worked behind the scenes to protect the church from the growing scandal.

Reverend Thomas Doyle, a canon lawyer who worked for the Vatican's Washington, DC embassy, in response to the action to remove Cardinal Mahony was quoted in that same article saying, "it revealed infighting between two highly placed church leaders, although the members of the

Roman Catholic hierarchy rarely broke ranks publicly."

The more interesting fact is that even though Cardinal Mahony was found guilty of the cover-up, the report noted an interesting irony. It states, "While Gomez's decision to strip Mahony of his administrative duties and reduce his public role was unprecedented in the American Roman Catholic Church, Mahony can still act as a priest, keep his rank as cardinal and remain on a critical Vatican panel that elects the next pope." I'm sure he was in Rome when the white smoke rose to announce the election of Pope Francis.

The records from individual rectories have been sealed due to the privacy act.

There are very few official records of any adultery charges against parish priests. According to a Springfield Republican article, "one priest was temporarily suspended after he admitted to an allegation by a housekeeper who became pregnant after several encounters with him. Her pregnancy ended in a stillbirth.

Because breaking vows with women over the age of eighteen was not a crime, there are no official records of either Father Brennan or any other priests in that diocese having such relationships.

There is now talk of priests being able to marry. I'm not sure that would have made a difference in my mother's affair. It's still hard to believe she lived and died in such a public way, yet secretly sheltered so much pain.

I will always feel that my dance with my mother ended before the music stopped. At least my understanding of her certainly did. So many questions were left unanswered.

But, of one thing I am certain. If I knew then what I know now, I would have gone to my mother's funeral.

ACKNOWLEDGMENTS

Special thanks to my beta readers, authors GeorgeAnn Jansson and Trilby Plants.

I am grateful for the continued support and encouragement from the members of the Coastal Authors Network of Pawleys Island, and the Carolina Forest Fiction Writers.

Without the efforts of the staff at the Belchertown Public Library, and the Deputy Assistant Commissioner, Victor Hernandez, of the Massachusetts Department of Developmental Services, this memoir could not have been completed.

The names and several locations in this memoir have been changed out of consideration for those persons who still live in the town and for those who have moved away but remain on this planet.

ABOUT THE AUTHOR

Trisha Moriarty is a pseudonym. The author has traded the long row of mills lining the canals in Massachusetts for the miles of beaches along the shore of the Carolinas. She and her husband are enjoying their retirement relaxing by the sea.